1001

HOUSE PLANT QUESTIONS ANSWERED

1001 HOUSE PLANT QUESTIONS ANSWERED

BY
STANLEY SCHULER

Drawings by Lombard C. Jones

FUNK & WAGNALLS
NEW YORK

First paperbound edition published 1968 by Funk & Wagnalls
Published by arrangement with D. Van Nostrand Company, Inc.

0–308–90078–2

PRINTED IN THE UNITED STATES OF AMERICA

12—76

How to Use this Book

"Will it grow well in my home?" you ask when you hear about a tempting new house plant.

"How do I grow it?" you ask when a neighbor gives you a house plant you have never heard of.

"How can I get it to bloom?" you ask when a healthy plant produces no buds.

"What's wrong?" you ask when one of your house plants suddenly goes limp.

The raising of house plants always brings up questions like these, and it is not because house plants are difficult and unaccommodating. My own feeling is that, by and large (there are obvious exceptions), they are most amenable. The fact that so many house plants are raised successfully in so many different—and often conflicting—ways and under so many different conditions proves this.

Nor do questions about house plants arise because they are unusually baffling plants. On the contrary, if you have a general idea how and where a given plant grows in nature, it is not too hard to figure out how it should be treated in the house.

I think we ask questions about house plants simply because we love them and need them to cheer our lives and our homes. After all, no one wonders or worries for long about something in which he has little interest.

This book has the hopeful aim of answering your questions about a large number of the most common house plants and some uncommon ones, too—thus making them even more of a pleasure than they already are. It is a book of how to grow, how to care for, how to get the most out of house plants.

The 258 general types and specific kinds of plants covered were selected for one or more of these reasons:

They are popular, widely grown plants, such as philodendron.

They are plants about which questions are often asked—African violets, for example.

They are excellent, generally available plants even though they may not be well known. Flame-of-the-woods is an example.

They are members of plant families, such as the gesneriads, which have become hobbies.

The book itself is divided into three sections: First, a section which answers questions about planting, growing, watering, protecting, and propagating house plants in general. Second, a section dealing with specific plants and their requirements. Finally, a brief section of useful lists telling where to grow, what to grow, and where to buy.

In using the book, you may find the question you have is not stated exactly as you may ask it. Don't let this frustrate you. If you glance through the questions that are presented, you will get your answer (provided your problem is not a highly individual one). For example, the specific question, "How should I pot up philodendron?" does not appear. But the answer is available in question No. 849: "Should a philodendron be repotted often?" and in question No. 846: "Why do the lower leaves of my philodendron dry out?"

In using the book, you will also find that one answer frequently refers to another. But even where there are no such cross-references, I urge you to look further than the answer given to your specific question. For example, if your question does happen to be, "Should a philodendron be repotted often?" you will find it helpful, after reading No. 849, to look back in Section 1 under "soil," "containers," and "potting methods." The information you get in these sub-sections will broaden your knowledge considerably.

In this book, in other words, one question supplements another, and each of the two main sections supplements the other. This makes for a manageable, not-too-bulky book that is crammed with information. And it also increases the book's usefulness to you.

Contents

Illustrations

SECTION **1**

General Culture of House Plants

SOIL

1. *Is there such a thing as an all-purpose potting soil?*

Plants have various soil preferences, and in cases where these are pronounced, special soil mixtures are suggested in Section 2 under the names of the plants. However, a good general-purpose mixture can be made by combining 2 parts loam, 1 part humus, and 1 part sand or vermiculite. Additions of small amounts of well-rotted manure and bone meal help to enrich the soil, but are not essential.

2. *Are the prepared potting soils sold in stores as good as homemade mixtures?*

Yes, and they save you the trouble of mixing your own. Most of them have been sterilized, too (see 16).

3. *What is loam?*

A soil composed of clay (less than 20 per cent), silt (30 to 50 per cent), and sand (30 to 50 per cent). Loam is excellent soil because it retains water and nutrients.

4. *How should very light, sandy loam be mixed to give potting soil a good consistency?*

Combine 2 parts loam with 1 part humus and ½ part sand.

Or combine 2 parts loam with 1½ or 2 parts humus and 1 part sand.

5. *What is the best way to lighten my heavy garden soil for pot use?*

Increase the amount of sand and humus mixed with it by about 50 per cent. In other words, combine 2 parts loam with 1½ parts humus and 1½ parts sand. If necessary, you can add even more humus and sand.

6. *What exactly is humus?*

Thoroughly decomposed vegetable matter, such as leaf mold, compost, or peat moss. Of these three, peat moss has the least nutritive value but is most generally used because it is so available.

7. *When is leaf mold ready for use in a soil mixture?*

When the leaves have decayed to a point where they crumble easily. They should be flaky, not caky or powdery.

8. *Does it make any difference what kind of sand I use in soil mixtures?*

Coarse or "sharp" sand generally found on river bottoms is preferred. This is the kind usually sold at masonry supply houses. Sea sand is often finer but, of course, it is salty. If used, it must be washed in fresh water for about fifteen minutes. Vermiculite and perlite are excellent substitutes for sand in potting mixtures.

9. *Does vermiculite have any advantages over sand?*

This micalike material, usually somewhat coarser than sharp sand, makes the soil mixture in which it is used more porous; it is also cleaner and much lighter in weight; and it is an excellent medium in which to sow seeds.

10. Can perlite be substituted for sand or vermiculite?

This lightweight, sterile, inert derivative of silica has good capacity to hold water and is a fine substitute for vermiculite or sand.

11. Why is charcoal sometimes used in potting soils?

To help prevent soil from souring, especially when plants are potted in undrained containers. Crushed charcoal may be mixed with the soil or small lumps placed in the bottom of the containers.

12. What kind of charcoal should I use in potting soil?

The kind sold for outdoor cooking is perfect. It can be used in lumps or crushed fine. Don't use charcoal briquets, which contain "binders."

13. How can I tell whether a soil is too acid or not acid enough?

Plants will not respond properly to soil that does not suit them. To be sure, send a sample of soil to your nearest agricultural experiment station for a free analysis. In fact, if you are mixing potting soil in sizable quantities and are uncertain about its acidity or alkalinity (pH), it is always a good idea to have a sample analyzed. A soil with a pH of 7 is said to be neutral; below that, it is acid; above that, alkaline. The pH scale ranges from 4 to 9. Most plants do well with a pH of 6 to 7.

14. What is the best way to make potting soil acid?

Use acid humus, such as leaf mold from oak or pine trees.

Or mix with the potting soil a little aluminum sulfate—about ½ teaspoonful to a 4-inch pot.

15. *Is peat moss acid? If so, when I am using it for humus, shouldn't I add lime to the soil mixture for plants that prefer a sweet soil?*

The types of peat moss on the market are acid in varying degrees, and it is difficult to find out exactly how acid they are. But don't let this bother you. Generally, they are not acid enough to affect most plants, and it is rarely necessary to add lime to potting mixtures just because they include peat moss.

16. *Should the soil for all house plants be sterilized?*

It is a good idea, especially for plants like African violets that are susceptible to root nematodes and fungous diseases.

17. *How do you sterilize soil?*

Here are three ways: (1) Moisten it and bake in a 200°F oven for two hours. If you need quantities, bake in a large bucket or drum over an outdoor fire. (2) Moisten and cook in a pressure cooker for twenty minutes at 15 pounds pressure. Remember, however, that any indoor cooking of soil is smelly. (3) Fumigate it with a volatile chemical—methyl bromide, ethylene dibromide, or chlorpicrin, which come under various trade names—in a tightly closed container such as a garbage can. Follow the manufacturer's directions carefully. Whatever method you use, wait two to three days before planting in the sterilized soil.

18. *When sterilizing soil, should I treat all ingredients of the mixture or just some of them?*

Soil, humus, sand, and manure should be sterilized. Such inorganic materials as vermiculite, charcoal, limestone, and superphosphate should not; add them to the mixture after the sterilizing.

19. *What is osmunda fiber and for what is it used?*

Osmunda fiber—sometimes called osmundine or orchid peat—comes from the fibrous roots of osmunda ferns. It is used instead of soil for orchids, bromeliads, and many other epiphytes (tree-perching plants).

20. *I have heard expert gardeners praise sphagnum moss. Why is it so wonderful and what is it used for?*

Sphagnum is a dried bog moss, very useful for: (1) Air layering (see 141). (2) As a soil medium for insectivorous plants, such as the Venus fly trap (see 985). (3) Sometimes as a substitute for osmunda in growing orchids and bromeliads. (4) Shredded fine, as an outstanding medium in which to sow seeds because it is sterile, holds moisture, and permits easy transplanting of seedlings. Of course, it will not sustain growth of plants for long unless nutrients are applied.

CONTAINERS

21. *What is the best container for house plants?*

There is a difference of opinion. Common red clay pots are generally considered best because they have bottom drainage holes and the porosity of the clay permits some air to reach the soil. But they are difficult to keep clean and require frequent watering. Painted clay pots and plastic pots also have bottom drainage, and they do not get encrusted with salts and dirt, but they permit no soil aeration. Glazed containers are the handsomest and easiest to clean, but they do not admit air to the soil, and most of them do not have drainage holes.

22. *Why is it important for soil to be aerated?*

Air circulating through the spaces around the soil particles promotes growth of roots and is important to the existence of soil organisms. A clay pot, being porous, admits a certain amount of air into the soil and therefore keeps the soil in better condition than does a nonporous pot. If you do use a nonporous pot, the soil can—and should—be aerated by light cultivation of the surface.

23. *Why is bottom drainage important?*

To prevent waterlogging of the soil. If their roots are constantly surrounded by moisture, plants receive no oxygen, and drown.

24. *If a container does not have a drainage hole, how do I provide drainage?*

Put a good layer of shards (broken pots), small stones, or hard cinders in the bottom. In small pots without bottom drainage, this layer should be 1 inch or more deep. In pots larger than 6 inches in diameter, the layer should be 2 to 3 inches deep.

25. *Do I need drainage material in a pot with a bottom hole?*

You need just enough to keep the soil from washing out. Place a good-sized, curved piece of pot directly over the drainage hole and then add from ½ to 1 inch of smaller pieces.

26. *What hanging containers are recommended for indoor use?*

Use solid containers of one sort or another. Moss-lined wire baskets are attractive, but they dry out fast and are difficult to water without making a mess in your house.

27. *What is a strawberry jar and what are good plants to grow in one?*

A strawberry jar is a very large, porous clay pot with small shell-shaped pockets protruding from the sides. Plants are set in the pockets as well as in the open top. Almost any small types of plants can be grown in a jar, but green training vines, such as ivy, and flowering trailers, such as some of the gesneriads—episcias, columneas, and some African violets—are ideal.

28. *Can I use tin cans as pots for house plants?*

Certainly. But they will rust if not well painted, and the soil in them can easily sour because air reaches it through only the top surface. The fact that house plants will grow in cheap tin cans indicates that they will grow in anything that holds soil. They are not particular about their abodes as long as you take care of them.

29. *What sizes do clay pots come in?*

The standard pots with depth equal to diameter are made in 1¾- to 14-inch diameters. Up to the 7-inch size, pots are available in fractional sizes; above that, they run 8, 9, 10, 12, and 14 inches.

30. *What is meant by azalea pots and cyclamen pots?*

Azalea pots are three-quarters the depth of standard pots. They come in sizes from 6 to 12 inches across. Cyclamen pots have five holes in the bottom instead of one. Sizes are limited to 5-, 6-, and 7-inch diameters. They are also three-quarters the depth of standard pots.

31. *What is a bulb pan?*

A red clay container half the depth of a standard flower

pot. Diameters range from 5 to 12 inches. Pans can be used not only for bulbs but also for other shallow-rooted plants, such as rex begonias, and for seedlings.

32. *How do you keep clay pots from developing nasty green scum and salty white crust on the outside?*

Scrub them regularly with a stiff brush and water. Use soap or scouring powder if necessary and rinse well afterwards.

33. *My house is very dry and I seem to have to water my plants all the time. Is there any way to cut down on this chore?*

Here are three ways to reduce evaporation: (1) Pot plants in nonporous containers. (2) Set each clay pot inside a rather tight-fitting glazed container, but be careful not to overwater. If you do, you're likely to create a stagnant pool in the bottom of the outer container and this may soak up into the clay pot and rot the roots. (3) Set each clay pot inside the next-size larger clay pot, and fill the space between with sphagnum moss which is kept damp.

34. *Won't I reduce loss of water from clay pots if I set them in jardinieres?*

You will but you may also kill your plants. Jardinieres are dangerous because they collect the water draining from the containers set into them and people often forget to empty them. As a result, the stagnant pool of water deepens until it reaches the set-in pot, which then soaks up the moisture, waterlogs the soil, and soon brings on root rot. If you must use jardinieres, put a block of wood in the bottom so the flower pot is above the water level. And empty the jardinieres regularly.

35. *How do you keep wooden tubs and window boxes from rotting out?*

Make them of redwood or cypress, both very resistant to decay. Other woods must be thoroughly treated with zinc or copper naphthanate (this one leaves a green stain). Do not use creosote or pentachlorophenol as a preservative; both harm plants. Liners of copper, heavy polyethylene film, or several layers of building paper also help prevent decay.

36. *I've had several wood tubs that worked fine until the bottoms warped and rotted. How can this be prevented?*

Raising a tub (or window box) off the floor an inch so that air can circulate underneath will help a lot. Support the container on casters, stones, or blocks of wood.

37. *Is there a way to make a big tub easier to move around? I have an avocado growing in one and it is awfully hard to lift and move outside in summer.*

You can handle this by mounting the tub on three or four casters or by boring 1½-inch holes through opposite sides of the tub near the top. Then a pipe can be temporarily inserted through the holes so that two men can easily carry the tub.

38. *How can I build a planter to serve as a low divider between our living and dining areas?*

Make it of wood, stone, brick, concrete—just about anything. A wood planter should be lined with copper. It's a good idea also to provide bottom drainage holes that carry excess water off into a removable tray under the planter. If you cannot do this, be sure to fill the bottom of the planter with 3 or more inches of coarse gravel. Or you can simply keep your plants in pots, set them in the planter, and surround them with peat moss.

39. *How should an indoor window box be built?*

Make it 6 inches deep; the width and length to fit a window sill. Provide one ¾-inch drainage hole for every 100 square inches of bottom surface if you can make some arrangement for catching and disposing of the runoff water. Otherwise, put 2 to 3 inches of gravel in the bottom. Construct the box of redwood or cypress to prevent decay.

40. *How do I make a metal plant tray for window plants?*

You may be able to buy a tray. If not, have a handyman make one out of sheet copper or galvanized iron. It should be about 1 inch deep, any width and length you need. Solder the corners so the tray will hold water. Then fill with ½ inch of white pebbles and set the pots on top. Keep water in the tray just to the surface of the pebbles—it will provide the humidity so many plants require.

41. *How do I prepare pots and other containers for planting?*

No matter what they are made of, used containers must first be washed thoroughly with soap and water to remove lingering microorganisms, and also to make them look better. New clay pots—as well as any not used for a long time—should be soaked in clear water for several hours; otherwise, they draw too much moisture from the soil.

42. *How can I grow house plants in sunny windows over radiators?*

If you must put them in such a place, cover the radiators with about 2 inches of insulating board or insulating fiber and then on top of this insulating material place a board or plant tray. The plants will grow well on top of this because they will be protected from excessive heat.

43. *What is the best way to make a window sill wide enough to hold potted plants?*

Just set a 6-inch board on top of or level with the sill and support it on large angle-irons or wood cleats fastened to the apron under the sill.

44. *Do I have to use glass for plant shelves built across a window at several levels?*

No, but it has some advantages: It looks better than solid shelves and is easier to keep clean. More important, when the sun is high in the sky, it lets the rays through to all the plants, and does not cut them off as wood shelves might. Use ¼-inch plate glass to support the weight of the pots, and be sure to have the front edges beveled and polished so you don't cut yourself.

POTTING METHODS

45. *What is the best way to pot a house plant?*

First, be sure the pot is clean and water-soaked (see 41). Dry it. Spread drainage material in the bottom and add enough soil to support the plant at the right level—about ½ to 1 inch below the pot rim. If the plant has a root-ball, fill in around it with soil, packing it to the firmness of the old soil. Smooth the surface and water. If the plant has bare roots, fill the pot about half full of soil, mounding it up a little in the center. Arrange the roots down over the mound and sift in new soil until the pot is full. Then firm the soil and water. (*Illustration 1*)

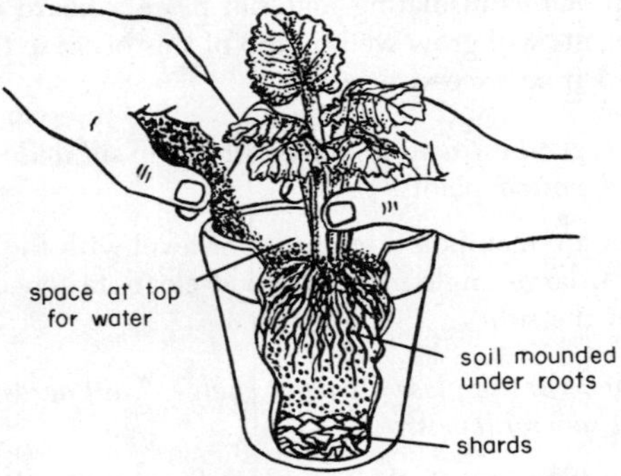

1. Potting a bare-rooted house plant

46. *When should house plants be repotted?*

When roots completely fill the pot. At this point the old soil has probably worn out and plant growth has slowed. You may be able to recognize this stage from the appearance of the plant, or roots may be growing out of the bottom of the pot. A sure test is to slide the root-ball out of the pot and examine it. If the surface of the root-ball is interlaced with roots, the plant needs repotting. This can be done at any time of year, but with mature plants it is generally best at the end of a resting period, just as new growth begins.

47. *When a plant needs repotting, how big should the new pot be?*

Just one size larger than the old pot. Avoid overpotting. Too much soil for too few roots is an unhealthy condition.

48. *The roots of some of my house plants crowd the pots but I have no room for larger pots. What should I do?*

Remove as much of the surface soil as you can without injuring the roots and replace it with fresh soil. This is the safest method. But you can knock the root-ball out of the pot, rub off excess soil, and put the plant back in the same pot but in new soil.

49. *What is meant by "hard-potting"?*

Hardwood plants, such as azaleas and camellias, are hard-potted; that is, the soil is packed very firmly around the roots. The packing is usually done with a stick of wood.

50. *Would repotting help plants that do not seem too healthy?*

If all else has failed, it might; but first check cultural requirements under the plant names in this book. If repotting is indicated, remove the plants from the pots, shake out the soil from the roots, and cut the roots back to healthy growth. Then replant in *smaller* pots. If you cut the roots back very hard, the foliage must also be pruned back (see 332).

WATERING

51. *How often should I water my house plants?*

It depends on the kind of plants, the extent of the root systems, the type of soil and container, the amount of sun, the atmosphere of the house, whether the plants are resting or growing actively. In other words, there is no definite answer. But for the majority of house plants, the general rule is to keep the soil barely moist but not soaking wet.

52. *How can I tell when plants need water?*

By feeling the soil. If it is dry to the touch and doesn't stick to your finger, apply water. For some plants, such as geraniums, water should be applied only when the soil feels completely dry. Then give them a good soaking. For other plants, such as African violets, the soil surface should never be allowed to dry completely. They need even, constant moisture, though not so much that the soil becomes waterlogged. Only a few plants such as dwarf banana require a really wet soil at all times.

53. *How much water should plants be given?*

For desert plants, see 364. The rules for *most* other plants are these: If you are watering them from above, apply water until it trickles out the bottom of the container. (Remove any excess after an hour or so.) If you are watering from the bottom, let the container stand in water until the surface soil is damp. In other words, when you water, be thorough; make sure that the soil is moistened through and through. With frequent small applications, soil is moistened only on top and stays dry below—a condition that destroys the deeper roots.

54. *What is the best time of day to water house plants?*

Practically, it makes little difference. Theoretically, it is better to water early in the day, because plants lose moisture more rapidly during daylight. It is also considered wise to apply water when the temperature is rising rather than falling.

55. *Should water for house plants be hot or cold?*

Some plants are not particular, provided the water is neither too icy nor too hot. Generally, room-temperature water —that is, lukewarm or tepid water—is safest.

56. *Is hard water bad for plants?*

It is not too good for plants that prefer acid soil. It may also cause thick, unsightly crusts of salts to form on red clay pots. In the case of African violets, it is thought that these salty crusts contribute to petiole rot (see 211).

57. *Is it better to water plants from the top or the bottom?*

Placing a pot up to half its depth in a bowl of water and letting it stay until the surface soil feels damp assures a somewhat better distribution of water through the soil than if you water from the top. It also assures that the deep roots of such plants as snake plant get adequate moisture. But it is usually easier to water plants most of the time from above; and if you don't use icy water and don't wet the foliage, you can do no harm even to such finicky plants as African violets.

58. *Shouldn't house plants really be watered from both top and bottom?*

Yes. Watering from the top is easier and helps to distribute fertilizer more or less evenly through the soil. Occasional watering from the bottom—by setting the pot in a bowl of water—helps to assure that the deep roots of plants also receive enough moisture.

59. *What is meant by "growing plants on the dry side"?*

Giving them less than their usual supply of water. In some cases, this means keeping the soil almost dry; in other cases, it means merely reducing the amount of moisture. Almost all plants are grown this way when they are resting. Some old-timers also use the phrase when they are referring to plants, such as geraniums, which are watered only when the soil surface becomes dry.

60. *How does wick-watering work?*

A glass-fiber wick is spread inside the pot on the bottom and is covered with soil (in this case, no coarse drainage material is used). The end of the wick is led out through the hole in the bottom and drawn into a container of water under the pot. As long as the container is kept filled, moisture is automatically carried up into the soil as it dries. Some have found this the ideal way to water potted plants; others consider that it does not save much work or assure better growth. (*Illustration 2*)

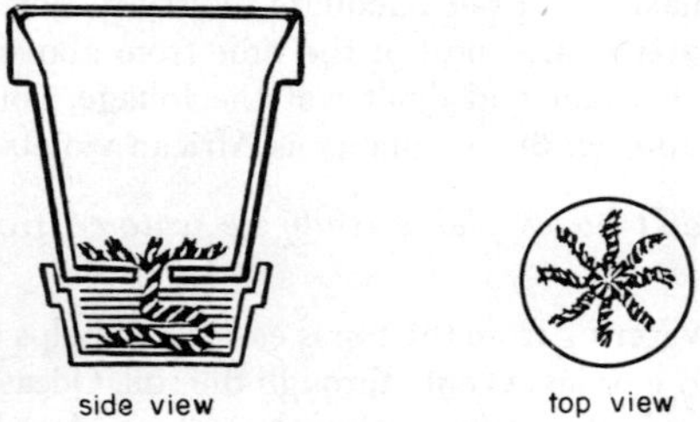

2. Wick watering

61. *Does it help to stand house plants out in the rain occasionally?*

This is an easy way to get the foliage clean. And plants seem to profit from the soft rain water—especially if you have had to use hard water most of the time. But driving rain may wreck a plant, and an outdoor temperature much lower than that of the house is sure to set it back.

FERTILIZING

62. *How often should house plants be fertilized?*

As a rough rule, every three weeks if they are growing well and are plants that require a very rich diet; every four weeks otherwise. It is better to underfertilize than to overfertilize. Do not feel that you must stick to a schedule. Be guided by the condition of the plant. And don't fertilize when a plant is in a period of rest. Follow the fertilizer manufacturer's advice as to amounts and frequency when you are using a commercial product.

63. *What is the best fertilizer for house plants?*

You can use any complete, or balanced, commercial fertilizer, but the easiest to use are those that come in liquid or soluble powder form. These are simply mixed in water and applied. Fertilizer formulas vary widely; but in general, any brand that has twice as much phosphorus as nitrogen and potash will be fine for most house plants. All three elements are needed.

64. *What do those numbers on fertilizer packages mean?*

The numbers (such as 10-15-10) denote the content of nitrogen, phosphorus, and potash. The first number always stands for nitrogen; the second, for phosphorus; the third, for potash.

65. *How good are plant tablets?*

They are very good, since they contain the three necessary elements for growth, and they are convenient to use. You can dissolve them in water according to the manufacturer's directions or simply insert one or more depending on size of plant into pencil-size holes in the soil close to the side of the pot. Every time you water the plant from above, a bit of the tablet dissolves.

66. *Most house-plant books recommend manure for fertilizing. Why do they?*

First, because many books were written before balanced commercial fertilizers were so widely available (or the books were written by people who were brought up using such fertilizers). Second, because manure *is* good fertilizer and also adds a lot of humus to the soil (which commercial fertilizers do not). However, manure is not easily come by today, and even dried kinds sold by garden stores smell. Furthermore, the amount of chemical elements provided varies among manures. In other words, manure is fine to use if you can get it. But for most growers of house plants, the balanced, inorganic fertilizers work better.

67. *Don't acid-soil plants, such as azaleas, require a special fertilizer?*

Yes, the fertilizer should have about equal amounts of nitrogen, phosphorus, and potash. For instance, acid-soil plants would prefer a 5-8-7 fertilizer to a 5-10-5.

68. *How can an extra amount of nitrogen or phosphorus or potash be given when a plant requires it?*

Just dilute the necessary element in water and apply. To give extra nitrogen, mix 1 tablespoon of nitrate of soda in 1 gallon of water. To give extra phosphorus, mix 1¼ tablespoons of superphosphate in 1 gallon of water. To give extra potash, mix 2 to 3 tablespoons of wood ashes in 1 gallon of water; but if the plants require an acid soil, mix 1 teaspoon of muriate of potash in 1 gallon of water instead of wood ashes.

69. *Why are my begonias so big and lush but producing very few flowers?*

They are getting too much nitrogen and need more phosphorus and potash. Nitrogen primarily encourages leaf and stem growth. Plant foods that have a high nitrogen content are excellent for foliage plants and for flowering plants with sickly foliage, but they may tend to discourage the blooming of healthy flowering plants.

70. *Are crushed eggshells in soil good for house plants?*

Some people strongly recommend eggshells as a way to give plants calcium, but a better source of calcium is finely ground limestone, such as you spread on the lawn.

71. *Should I feed house plants Vitamin B_1?*

Despite the claims made for B_1, there is no concrete evidence that it helps plants.

72. *Should house plants growing in water be fertilized?*

Yes. Use a complete plant food that contains—in addition to nitrogen, phosphorus, and potash—iron, boron, manganese, and zinc.

LIGHT REQUIREMENTS

73. *Which are the best windows for house plants?*

It depends on whether they need full sun (as most flowering plants do), partial sun (as some flowering and many foliage plants do), or simply ample light (which suits a few flowering plants and almost all foliage types). None thrives in the dark. South windows are the brightest and admit sun for the better part of the day. East windows are excellent, giving cool morning sun for three to four hours. West windows admit as much sun as east windows, but the sun's heat in the afternoon is harmful to some plants. Unobstructed north windows give a cool, even light but no sun. You can have a fine garden in any fully lighted window provided you select the proper plants. (See Section 3, Useful Lists.)

74. *Since I moved from the North into the deep South, am I right in thinking that the recommendations I used to follow for growing house plants in a sunny south window no longer apply?*

Yes and no. A plant that needs sun to grow needs it in the South (or Southwest) as well as in the North. But because the sun in the South rides higher in the sky and is hotter, a plant growing in a south window in the deep South may get more sun than it likes and be burned. For instance, in the North, orchids should be placed in a south window and exposed to sun all day long except in spring and summer, when midday shading is required. In the South, however, orchids must be protected from the midday sun the year round (see 794). You are right in suspecting that exposures recommended for northern house plants may be harmful to southern house plants, but there are no simple rules for figuring the difference. If you know that a plant is finicky about sunlight to some degree, just watch it carefully. If it is getting too much sun, its yellow or bleached look will soon show that it dislikes conditions.

75. *How can I tell if my plants are getting enough light?*

If they are getting enough, they will make strong, bushy growth and produce plenty of flowers. If they are not, stems will grow lanky and soft and leaves will be thin, pale, and rather sparse.

76. *Can house plants get too much sun?*

Definitely. African violets are notable examples of plants that react badly to strong sunlight, but there are many others whose leaves also get bleached, yellowish, and out of shape with too much sun.

77. *Exactly what do people mean when they say a plant needs "full sun"?*

They mean that it needs five or more hours of sun a day. This you can get only in a south window.

78. *What is the difference between partial and filtered sun?*

There are different opinions, but generally, partial sun means anything less than five hours of sun a day. Filtered sun means sun that is filtered through a light curtain the equivalent of about two layers of cheesecloth or through the leaves of overhanging trees.

79. *What plants shall I grow to get long or continuous bloom in a very sunny window?*

Few plants give truly continuous bloom but those that come close to it in a south window are crown of thorns, the reed epidendrum orchids, firecracker vine, lantana, little pickles, marguerite, patience, pomegranate, and shrimp plant.

80. *Can I get continuous or extended bloom in an east window with two to three hours of sun a day?*

You can get consistent—if perhaps not quite continuous—bloom from African violets, wax begonias, flamingo flower, spathifyllum, streptocarpus, and sweet olive.

81. *How can I keep my plants from growing toward the light?*

You cannot prevent heliotropism, as this natural phenomenon is called. But you can prevent one-sided growth by turning the pots halfway around every day or so.

82. *Is it safe to grow sun-loving house plants in full sun outdoors?*

It is always safe to grow them in sun filtered through a high, open tree, and it is usually safe to grow them in full sun provided that you let them adjust gradually to the increased light. The problem is that the light intensity within even the sunniest south window is much lower than that outdoors. So if you move plants directly from the house into full sun, you are likely to shock them so badly that they go to pieces. You should, instead, move them first into light shade, then into partial sun, and finally into full sun. Do this over a period of three to four weeks.

83. *Should flowering plants from the florist be put in a sunny window?*

If they are in full flower, no; it will shorten the length of bloom. But if they are mostly in bud, give them as much sun as you can (provided, of course, that they are not African violets, begonias, or other plants that need only partial sun).

84. *What are the advantages of growing plants under electric light?*

Electric light makes up for natural-light deficiencies resulting from dim windows, dull weather, and the simple fact that indoor light never equals outdoor light. Electric light added to daylight, or electric light alone, produces better growth and flowering and makes it possible to grow plants even in a dark basement.

85. *Which types of lamps are used for growing plants indoors?*

You can use fluorescent lamps alone or fluorescents supplemented by a small (25-watt) incandescent bulb. If you use ordinary fluorescents, the addition of a small incandescent bulb helps to promote better growth because it gives off the red rays that plants require. But if you use the new Gro-Lux fluorescent tubes—made especially for the indoor gardener—you need nothing else.

86. *I have had plants growing in a northeast window under two 20-watt fluorescent tubes, but they have not done especially well. Why not?*

Undoubtedly the 20-watt tubes helped to improve the poor exposure, but the foot-candles of illumination they produced were not enough to stimulate strong growth and bloom. You need four 20-watt tubes or two 40's to produce enough foot-candles to encourage best flowering in most plants; and many gardeners use twice as many lights to achieve maximum results.

87. *Where are lights placed in relation to plants?*

Lights are hung directly above, the distance from the fluorescent tubes varying from 6 to 15 inches depending on the size and type of plants. With adjustable chains, lights can be moved up and down as necessary to control growth. Incandescent lights must be hung higher—at least 24 inches above plants—because they give off a great deal of heat which may be harmful. Fluorescents, on the other hand, are "cool" lights. (*Illustration 3*)

88. *How many hours of artificial light do plants require per day?*

This varies with the plants and the season of the year. In general, plants require a total of twelve to eighteen hours of light a day to bloom. Therefore, you need electric light only long enough to make up the difference between the total light required by a plant and the length of the day. For instance, if you are growing gloxinias, which require a total of about four-

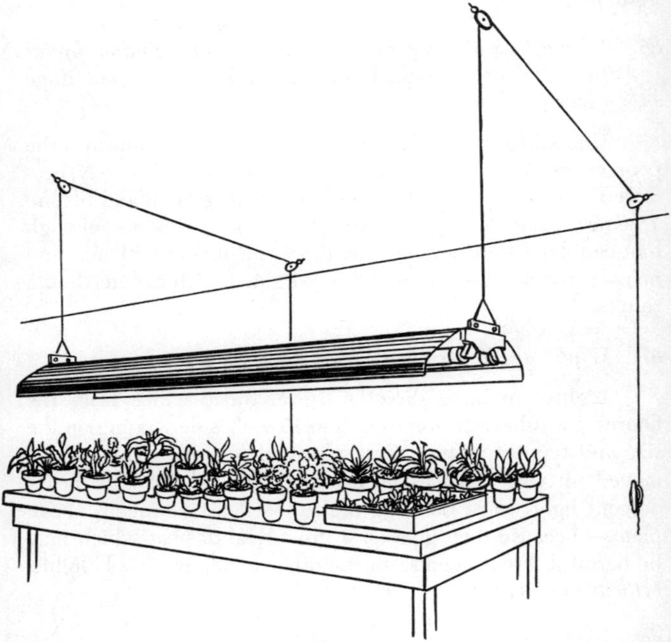

3. Set-up for growing plants under fluorescent light

teen hours, and if in January daylight lasts only nine hours, keep the fluorescents on for five hours.

89. *If plants grow better under electric light, why not keep the lights on twenty-four hours a day?*

Growth is dependent on darkness as well as on light. If you give plants more light than they require, you will actually retard growth.

ATMOSPHERIC REQUIREMENTS

90. *What is the best temperature for house plants?*

Most house plants do well at 68° to 70°F during the day, with a drop—as in nature—to 55° to 60°F at night. Temperatures much higher or lower are generally harmful, but some plants (such as cyclamen, primrose, and strawberry geranium) require lower-than-average house temperatures—even down to 50°F in the daytime.

91. *In severe weather, I notice that the air just inside the windows where I grow my plants is very cold though the room is warm. Will this hurt the plants?*

It certainly will. You would be wise to install storm windows to keep out the cold, or move the plants in somewhat from the glass, or put a shield of newspaper between glass and plants, or hang a couple of incandescent lamps (which give off quite a lot of heat) next to the glass over the plants.

92. *What is the easiest way to raise house humidity for plants that require a lot?*

Fill saucers with ½ inch or more of pebbles and set the potted plants on top. Keep the saucers filled with water to just below the surface of the pebbles. Other ways to increase humidity are to spray plants lightly with water once or twice a day, or set pans of water among them or, preferably, on radiators nearby. A fine source of humidity is your clothes dryer, if you can figure out a way to exhaust the moisture from it into the room where you grow those plants which most need humidity—and if you don't ruin the paint in the process!

93. *What is a good sprayer to use for misting house plants?*

The Flit-gun type delivers a fine mist adequate for providing humidity but not for dislodging insects. The Larvex-bottle type with a nozzle that pumps up and down and the bulb-type that works when you squeeze a rubber bulb give harder, coarser streams. Any of these are fine for misting a small number of plants, but if you have a lot of plants, a pressure sprayer like that used in the garden is easier and also does a better all-round job. Whatever sprayer you use, it's a good idea—if you value the appearance of your house—to set the plants in a sink or tub before misting them. Leave them there until the foliage dries.

94. *Is it necessary to let fresh air into rooms where plants grow?*

Yes, fresh air is required for the good health of most house plants, but do not let cold blasts strike them. In very cold weather, ventilate indirectly through an adjoining room.

95. *Is it true that house plants can be killed by gas fumes in the air?*

Many are extremely sensitive to manufactured gas and can even be killed by it, but the best available evidence indicates that they are not harmed by natural or bottled gas, the types in almost universal use today.

PRUNING AND TRAINING

96. *Should house plants be pruned?*

By all means if you want growth that is neat, orderly, and

in the proper direction. With some plants, pruning is also necessary to assure continuous growth and bloom.

97. *How should house plants be pruned?*

Use a sharp knife or pruning shears. If you are taking back a branch, cut just above a leaf or leaf bud. If a branch is to be removed entirely, cut as close as possible to the main branch. How much growth you remove depends on the needs of the plant and your own thoughts about its appearance.

98. *How often is it safe to prune house plants?*

If you take off a little growth at a time, you can prune frequently—every month or even every couple of weeks if a plant is a fast grower. Very frequent pruning is necessary to shape bonsai (see 331-332). But some slow growers can go unchecked for a year or two. You have to gauge pruning to the development and type of the plant.

99. *How do you prevent young plants from getting tall and scraggly?*

By pinching off the tips of one or more of the growing shoots, thus forcing out side shoots.

100. *One of my begonias growing in an east window was lanky, so I pinched off the shoots to force it to bush out. A couple of new branches finally appeared, but did not grow much; and the old shoots got lanky again. How can I get more bushy growth?*

Pinching back is right but your plant probably needs more sunlight. Plants that need considerable sunshine or bright light to develop well do not respond sufficiently to pruning unless also given the proper exposure.

101. Should house plant roots be pruned frequently?

No, unless you are trying to check top growth (see 331).

102. Is it safe to root-prune a plant and not prune the foliage?

No. Root and top must be in balance. If the foliage is heavy and the roots have been severely reduced, the plant will probably wilt and die.

103. What is the best support for climbing vines?

Use whatever suits your needs: a wood lattice, a strip of chicken wire, strings, wires, bamboo stakes, etc. Just watch out that the full-grown vine does not become top-heavy. You can counteract the tendency to top-heaviness by planting in a large container or by fastening supports to a window frame or wall.

104. What kind of support do philodendrons need to climb?

Philodendrons, like pothos, wax plant, and a number of other favorite vines, climb by means of little aerial roots which cling to rough surfaces. The support most commonly used for them is a length of red cedar with the bark left on. Any rough wood will do as well. So will a smooth stake wrapped in moss or osmunda fiber. Be sure to sink whatever you use all the way to the bottom of the container and pack it in with soil. Otherwise it may topple over under the weight of the plant.

INSECTS, DISEASES, AND OTHER AILMENTS

105. What is a contact insecticide?

A material used to get rid of sucking insects such as aphids and spider mites. Malathion is one of the best, but there are many others: DDT, chlordane, lindane, and nicotine. While some have a residual effect and will also kill insects that chew foliage, all are more effective when they actually *strike* the insects. So it's important when using them to spray or dust every part of a plant.

106. *What is a fungicide?*

A chemical applied as a spray or a dust to control and prevent fungous diseases such as mildew and botrytis. Many good fungicides are available, but none will control every disease. Always apply according to the manufacturer's directions and be sure that you cover the underside as well as the top of the leaves.

107. *What makes the foliage of some of my plants turn yellow?*

They may not be getting enough nitrogen from the soil. You may be over- or underwatering, or giving too much sun. Or heat may be too high. African violet leaves may turn yellow if they are wet with cold water. Yellowing is also caused by insects or disease. Check all the possibilities, because yellowing foliage is a sure sign of some trouble.

108. *The leaves of my geraniums are pale and yellowish, and some have bronzy speckles. What is causing this?*

Probably spider mites. These are so small you can hardly see them except with a magnifying glass, but they do serious damage to a number of plants. Since they thrive in a dry, hot atmosphere, discourage them by humidifying the air or spraying the plants forcibly with water once or twice a week. But if the infestation is established, you ought to spray every week for three weeks with malathion or some other miticide. Sodium selenate treatment of the soil also cleans up or prevents mites (see 110-111).

109. *What is causing the sticky substance on my African violets? Some leaves are also covered with a black mold and are out of shape.*

Aphids or plant lice are the cause. These are tiny, soft, sucking insects, usually greenish but sometimes red or black. They attack a number of different plants but are easily controlled with malathion or lindane sprays; or you can eliminate them by treating the soil with sodium selenate (see 110-111).

110. *What is sodium selenate and how is it used?*

Sodium selenate is a poison which is applied to soil, absorbed by plant roots, and taken up into stems and leaves. When sucking insects, such as mites, feed on poisoned leaves, they die. Sodium selenate is best applied by setting a pot in a solution until the soil has been wet through. One treatment should take care of a plant for about five months (see 111).

111. *Can sodium selenate kill plants as well as insects?*

A strong solution can harm or even kill plants. What is known as the Standard Solution (1 gram to 1 gallon of water) is generally considered dangerous for such tender plants as African violets and is not recommended for them unless the plants have got to a kill-or-cure condition. The Extra Dilute Solution (¼ gram to 1 gallon of water) is much safer and effective if four doses are given at weekly intervals.

112. *What gets rid of the small, whitish, hard lumps on the leaves and stems of my house plants?*

The lumps are scale insects. They are often white, but may be gray or brown. When the insects are young and actively moving around (which isn't very often), they can be controlled with malathion spray applied two or three times at weekly intervals. But when they are mature, settle down on a leaf or stem and develop their hard, scaly armor, such treatment is ineffective. The best thing is to rub them off carefully with a cloth soaked in soapy water.

113. *How do I control the little, oval, waxy white insects that appear on house plants?*

These obnoxious insects are mealy bugs. They can be removed from plants with a cotton swab dipped in alcohol if there are not too many of them. For severe infestations, apply a malathion spray. Mealy bugs suck plant juices and produce a "honeydew" on which fungi may grow.

114. *I have several different kinds of plants that look deformed, especially in the center. Leaves are distorted and brittle, flower stems stunted. What is causing the trouble? I can't see anything on the plants.*

Probably cyclamen mites, which are invisible without a magnifying glass. They attack a number of plants besides cyclamens, especially African violets. Badly infested plants should be destroyed. Others can be sprayed frequently with malathion. But to put a permanent end to mites—or at least to stop them for a long time—treat with sodium selenate (see 110-111).

115. *How can I stop an infestation of white flies?*

These small sucking insects that attack the undersides of leaves and cause yellowing and wilting can be controlled by spraying with DDT or malathion. Several sprayings with a nicotine-soap solution are also effective. Be sure the spray strikes the undersides of the leaves.

116. *Do springtails damage house plants?*

Not as far as is known but they are a nuisance. You can get rid of them by dusting the soil with chlordane.

117. *How can I recognize root-knot nematodes on house plants?*

Plants look listless, do not grow, may actually get smaller. Small knots may be visible at the base of stems. The roots will be brown at the tips and show small knots or lumps.

118. *What can be done for house plants attacked by root-knot nematodes?*

Nothing. Destroy them. Throw out the soil in an area where you are not gardening. Scald the containers before using them again.

119. *Why have the stems of one of my anemones rotted just above the soil?*

This sounds like crown rot, a fungous disease that attacks some plants, especially when they are set so low in the soil that water settles in and around the crowns instead of draining away from them. About all you can do once the rot starts is to dig up the plants, salvage the unaffected portions and dip them in bichloride of mercury solution; then replant. To prevent crown rot, use sterilized soil and set the plant crowns higher than the surrounding soil.

120. *How can I check mildew?*

Pick off the mildewed leaves and destroy them. Dust the plants with sulfur or spray with phaltan. Mildew thrives when temperatures are high and the air humid. It may be a serious problem on house plants moved outdoors in summer.

121. *What causes yellow spots on the leaves of plants that are growing well?*

Any number of things resulting from poor culture or from mysterious causes we know nothing about. If only a few leaves are spotted, the plant will not be harmed, but if the leaf-spot is general, then the plant may die. Pick off spotted leaves and destroy them. Be careful not to overwater or splash leaves. Check room temperature to be sure it is not too hot for good plant health.

122. *Are worms good for potted plants? I understand that they help in a garden.*

Worms disturb the roots of potted plants and so tunnel the soil that it dries out quickly. Unpot plants and dig out the worms, or force them to the surface by watering with a solution of ¼ teaspoon dry mustard in water.

REST PERIODS, SUMMER AND VACATION CARE

123. *What is meant by the "rest periods" of plants?*

These are times when plants go to sleep or become dormant or simply slow down. Some plants, such as bulbs, die down. Some lose their leaves. Others just stop growing or blooming.

124. *When do plants have rest periods?*

Different plants rest at different times of the year. Usually their rest periods indoors correspond to their rest periods when they are growing outdoors in their natural abodes.

125. *How should I handle house plants during rest periods?*

Proper care during this period varies according to the

type of plant, but in general, reduce the water supply, stop fertilizing, and keep plants somewhat cooler than usual.

126. *Is it advisable to put house plants outdoors in the summer?*

Almost all house plants thrive on a summer outdoors. African violets are a notable exception, although some people put them outside without ill effects.

127. *How should house plants be treated when moved outdoors in summer?*

Place them in shade, partial shade, or sun according to their natures (see 82). Protect fragile specimens from hard rain, strong wind, and dogs. You can set the plants on the floor of the porch or terrace or in plant stands. Or you can

4. How to plunge pots outdoors in summer

sink the pots of upright plants in the ground, but in this case be sure to set them on a thick layer of gravel or hard cinders (*Illustration 4*). Water regularly; don't depend on rain. Guard against pests and diseases.

128. *What is meant by "plunging" a pot?*

Sinking it into the soil of a garden bed, usually up to its rim. Don't do this, however, until first making a bed of gravel for it to stand on (see 127).

129. *How should I take care of house plants when I go on vacation?*

In summer, plunge in the garden the pots of all those that can be moved outside. Water well. In winter, remove flowers and buds which sap the plants' energy. Do not lower house temperature too much. Before you leave, water plants well, and if you are to be gone several weeks, set the pots in a box of sphagnum moss so they will not dry out fast. Enclose those plants which require a lot of humidity in a tent of polyethylene film, but leave this a bit loose so air can get in to discourage fungi. Of course, the safest way to care for your plants is to ask a neighbor to keep an eye on them. Leave instructions.

PROPAGATING

130. *When is the best time to root house-plant cuttings?*

In general, in the spring and early summer. Select stems not in flower and neither soft nor tough. If they snap when bent double, they are usually about right. Take cuttings from the tips of growing shoots, preferably those rising from the base of the plant.

131. *How much of a stem should be used for a cutting?*

From 2 inches for small plants to 6 inches for large ones; 4 inches is a good average. Cut the stems about ¼ inch below a leaf, and cut off the leaves from the lower third of the stem. (*Illustration 5*)

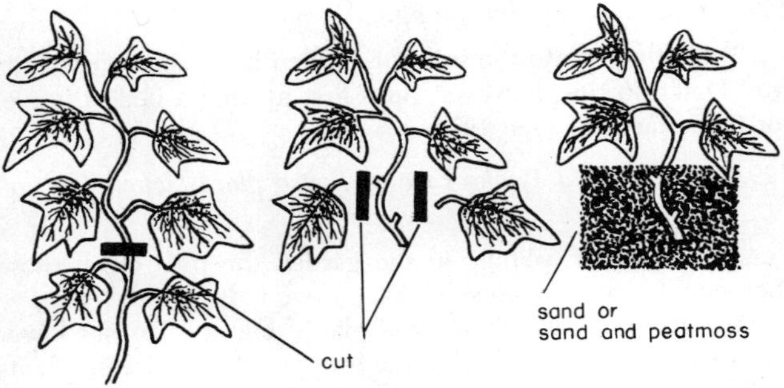

5. How to make a stem cutting

132. *What do stem cuttings root best in?*

Sand alone or a half-and-half mixture of sand and peat moss. Keep either one damp until roots develop.

133. *Why do the slips I try to root just shrivel up and die?*

Your cuttings may be succumbing to lack of moisture in the air. Experiments show that most cuttings root more quickly in a humid atmosphere. To be sure of humidity, use a propagating case that you can buy or approximate by covering your pot or flat of cuttings with polyethylene film. Don't let this touch the cuttings. Drape it over wire hoops or croquet wickets and draw it down under the bottom of pot or flat. This film holds in moisture and prevents wilting. (*Illustration 6*)

134. *Is it true that only polyethylene film should be used to cover flats of cuttings?*

No, any plastic film will do and so will glass, but polyethylene is strong, easy to handle and can also transmit air

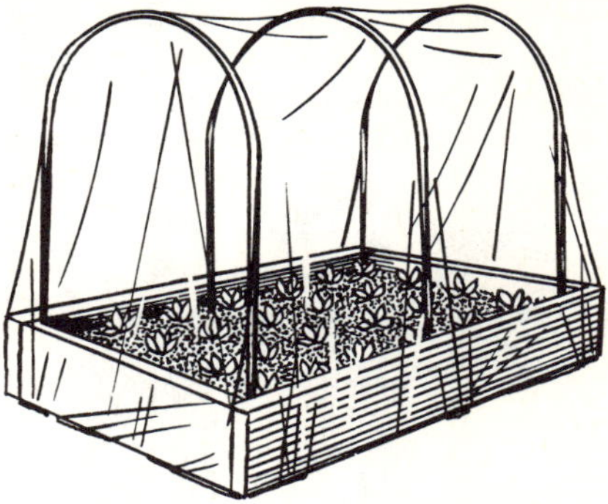

6. Propagating stem cuttings under polyethylene film

but not water vapor. This means that cuttings under it are bathed in vapor yet are also exposed to a small amount of fresh air from the outside. Even with polyethylene you can get mildew on cuttings (though to a lesser extent than with other films). On this account, be sure to remove the film completely for about fifteen minutes every day. And it is advisable to spray cuttings with a fungicide every week.

135. Do cuttings root faster if propagated under electric light?

Yes. Use the lights as suggested in 86-87, but note that while cuttings take kindly to electric light, they should not be exposed to direct sunlight.

136. What is the pot-in-pot method of propagating house plants?

This is an easy way to propagate a small number of plants. Fill a pot or bulb pan 8 inches or more in diameter with sand or a sand and peat moss mixture. In the center sink a

3-inch pot with the drainage hole corked. Insert the cuttings in the sand. Keep the small pot filled with water. It will supply sufficient moisture to the sand and you won't have to worry about watering the cuttings so often. (*Illustration* 7)

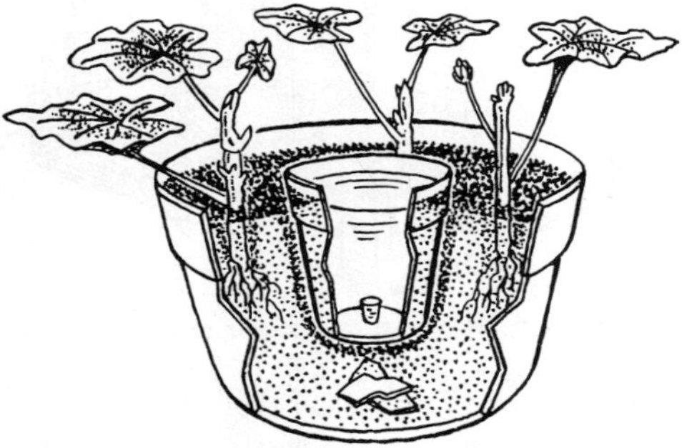

7. Pot-in-pot method of propagating cuttings

137. Do hormones improve the rooting of stem cuttings?

Yes, for most plants. All you have to do is dip the end of the stem (or a leaf-stem) into the hormone and insert it in the rooting medium. Follow the manufacturer's directions.

138. What house-plant cuttings can be rooted in a glass of water?

Among others, philodendron, geranium, begonia, coleus, English ivy, oleander, wandering Jew, Chinese evergreen, pandanus. Cover a wide-mouthed tumbler with perforated wax paper and insert stems through the holes to support leaves above the water and also to retard evaporation. A narrow-necked bottle provides similar support and also reduces evaporation. Give more water as the supply goes down in the receptacle. (*Illustration 8*)

8. Propagating a leaf cutting in water

139. What is a half-ripe wood cutting?

This is a cutting of a shoot that has stopped growing but has not yet matured. It is usually taken in late summer.

140. From which house plants can leaf cuttings be made?

African violets, gloxinias, snake plant, kalanchoe, pick-a-back plant, rex begonia, peperomia, sedums, echeveria are commonly propagated this way. Some of these can be started in water only. All can be rooted in damp sand or sand and peat moss. The usual method is to cut off a leaf with about 1 inch of stem and insert the stem in the sand; then cover the pot or box with polyethylene film. But special steps are taken with some plants, such as snake plant and rex begonia.

141. What kind of cuttings do I take from a rubber plant that has grown too big for my sun porch?

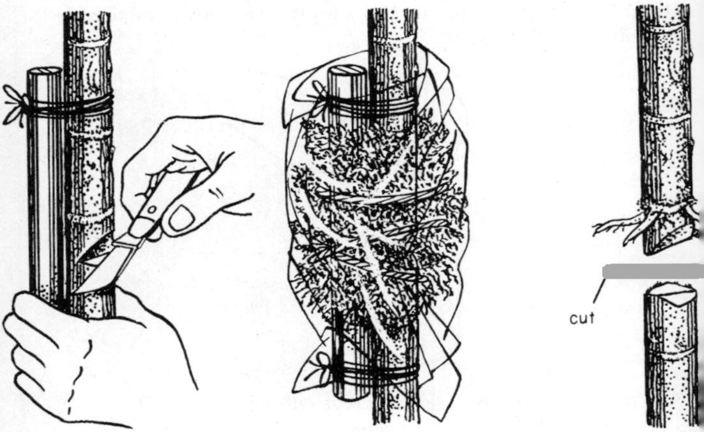

9. How to air-layer a plant

It is much better to air-layer the plant than to make cuttings, which will take a long while to develop. Air-layering is a method often used for propagating rubber plant, dracaena, dumb cane, monstera, croton, and other large plants. To make an air-layer, cut a notch in the stem 2 to 6 inches below the tip and brace the stem with a wood splint. Wrap the cut place in wet sphagnum moss and overwrap with polyethylene film. Remove film and wet the sphagnum often enough to keep it damp until roots develop at the cut. This takes eight weeks or so. Then remove the moss, cut off the stem below the roots, and pot the new plant in soil. Air-layering kits are available at garden-supply stores. (*Illustration 9*)

142. *Can house plants be propagated by burying the long stems in soil as you do ivy outdoors?*

Many trailing and climbing plants, as well as those that send out runners like the strawberry geranium, can be propagated this way. Just hold down a stem or runner on the soil surface at a joint. You can weight it with a stone or fasten with a hairpin. Cover the joint with a little soil. This is called stem-layering. (*Illustration 10*)

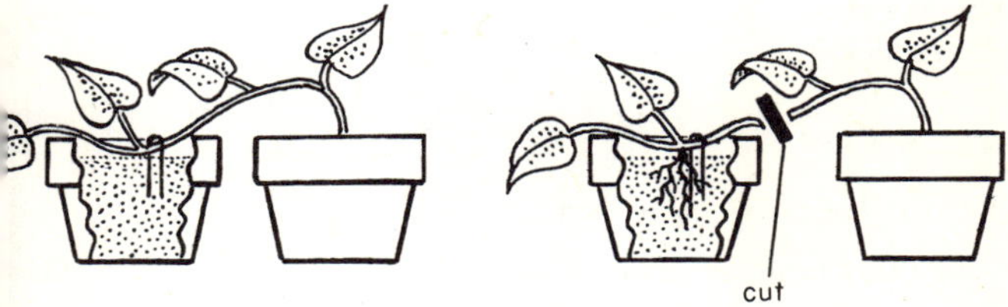

10. Propagating a plant by stem-layering

143. Can I remove and grow a section from an African violet that seems to have divided into two plants?

Plants such as African violets that often make many offsets are easily propagated by division. Handle carefully when separating them. You will probably need a knife to cut them apart. Be sure to take some roots with each new plant.

144. How are house plants grown from seed?

Sow the seeds in pots or flats of sterilized soil, sphagnum moss, vermiculite, or other sterile medium. Press the seeds in lightly. Cover large seeds with just a sprinkling of soil. Set the flats or pots in room-temperature water until the soil surface feels damp. Then cover with glass or polyethylene film and set in a warm, shaded place indoors or out depending on time of year. To hasten germination, place containers under fluorescent lamps or over gentle heat.

145. *Although I dusted seeds with a disinfecting powder to prevent damping-off, only a few germinated. Why was this?*

Seed disinfectants are good but not sure-fire preventives of damping-off. In fact, some experts feel that too much disinfectant prevents germination. You can avoid damping-off almost entirely by sowing seeds in sterile soil, sphagnum moss, or vermiculite.

BULB FORCING

146. *What is meant by "forcing" bulbs?*

Making them bloom ahead of their normal season. Bulbs are not the only plants which are forced; many others, such as azaleas and hydrangeas, are also pushed ahead of schedule by adjusting temperature, light, and moisture.

147. *Which spring bulbs can be forced for indoor bloom?*

Daffodils, tulips, hyacinths, crocuses, glory-of-the-snow, grape hyacinths, snowdrops, scilla, some iris. Certain varieties are better for forcing than others. For details, consult each group.

148. *When should spring bulbs be planted for forcing? For a succession of bloom, should I plant them at different times?*

Plant any time in the fall and put them all in at the same time. The date of planting does not control the date of flowering (see 151).

149. *How should spring bulbs be planted for forcing?*

Plant in clay pots—5-inch size for a single exhibition-size hyacinth bulb; 6-inch or larger for a number of standard-size bulbs. Use general-purpose potting soil (see 1). Set bulbs so tips just show at the soil surface. Space several bulbs for one pot about 1 inch apart. Water thoroughly. Set in a cold place.

150. *How are forcing bulbs handled during their cold-storage period?*

After bulbs are potted, the easiest method is to store them in a dark corner of a basement or garage where the temperature is 35° to 45°F (it should not be warmer nor go below freezing). Cover with burlap. Don't let soil dry out; keep just slightly damp. Another method is to set the pots in a 12- to 15-inch-deep trench with a bottom layer of hard cinders or gravel. Spread sand on top of pots to keep them clean. Then fill in around them with soil, mounding it over them. When the soil first freezes, cover with hay or evergreen boughs to prevent further freezing. A variation of the second method is to set pots outdoors in a box. Fill in around and over them with damp peat moss. Cover the entire box with straw when freezing weather hits.

151. *When can bulbs be brought out of cold storage?*

As soon as they have filled the pots with roots. This takes six weeks or so. About this time you can check root growth by lifting out one pot. Slide the root-ball of earth out of the pot. The lower surface of the ball should now be covered with roots and the bulb ready for forcing. But pots can stay in cold storage as long as you like after roots are formed. Plants will not make much top growth until brought indoors. You can plant a number of bulbs at the same time and still get a succession of bloom. After roots are formed, bring the pots indoors one or two at a time at ten- to fourteen-day intervals. (*Illustration 11*)

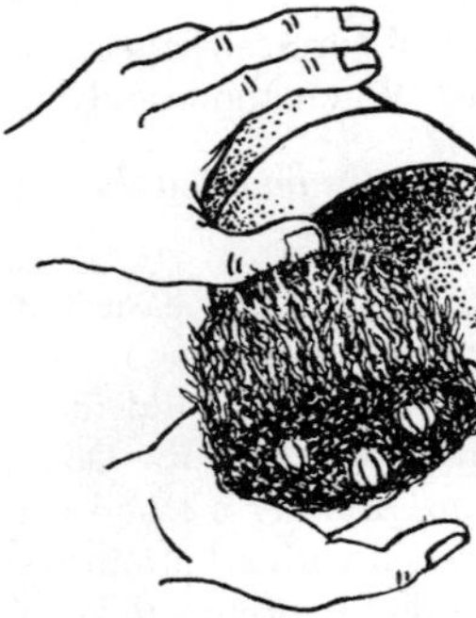

11. How to check root growth when forcing bulbs

152. How are bulbs handled when they are brought in from cold storage?

Hold them in a dark, cool (about 50°F) place for about three weeks until leaves and flower stalks are 6 to 8 inches high. Water moderately. Then bring them inside, first to the light, then to a sunny window that is not too warm. A temperature of 60° to 70°F is about right. During leaf and stalk formation, growth will be yellow because of lack of light. Do not worry about this. It will quickly green up when exposed to light.

TERRARIUMS AND DISH GARDENS

153. How do I make a terrarium?

Select any glass container: a fish bowl, a large open-mouthed jar or bottle, or a brandy snifter. Get a sheet of glass to put on top. To prevent waterlogging and souring of the soil, cover the bottom of the container with 1 inch of sand mixed with lumps of charcoal. Over this spread 2 to 5 inches of a general-purpose soil mixture (see 1).

154. What plants are suitable for a terrarium?

Almost all small plants that enjoy high humidity, especially tropical plants, wild woodland plants, insectivorous plants, mosses, and little ferns.

155. How is a terrarium managed?

Water sparingly and only when the soil begins to dry out. (As long as moisture condenses on the inside of the glass, no water is required.) Ventilate by removing the glass for a little while or just sliding it off a crack if the inside looks steamy. Keep in good light but not in sunlight, which might scorch foliage and cause excessive fogging of the glass. Attractive terrariums can be grown under fluorescent light.

156. How are dish gardens planted?

For containers, use glass or ceramic—but not metal—bowls at least 3 inches deep, with or without drainage holes. Put in the bottom a 1-inch layer of gravel, cover with a thin layer of moss to keep the soil from settling, and then fill to within ½ inch of the top with general-purpose soil (see 1).

157. Which plants are recommended for dish gardens?

Cacti and succulents are favorites, but you can grow almost anything from flowering and foliage plants to seedling trees and shrubs.

158. *How can I manage a dish garden that was given to me with a mixture of desert and tropical cacti and succulents?*

You can't: they won't thrive together. Separate the two types of plants. Make the dish garden entirely of desert or entirely of tropical plants. You can pot the extras individually.

SECTION **2**

How to Grow Specific House Plants

Plants are listed alphabetically under the names by which they are most widely known. Some are identified by their botanical names—as, *Bougainvillea glabra* (paper flower); some by their most popular common name—as, Babys-tears (*Helxine solieroli*). All plants may be found in the Index under both botanical and common names.

ABELIA GRANDIFLORA EDWARD GOUCHER

Small long-blooming hybrid shrub with clusters of pink flowers and lustrous leaves in summer

159. *What are the best growing conditions for an abelia indoors?*

Use general-purpose soil (see 1) and keep it evenly and constantly moist, but not wet. Grow the plant in a sunny window in a cool (45° to 60°F) room. Propagate by green-wood cuttings in summer.

ACACIA

Large genus of tropical trees and shrubs with feathery foliage and clusters of bright yellow flowers in March and April

160. *Why is it so difficult to grow acacia indoors?*

Mainly because the required growing conditions are found in so few houses. Acacias need a winter temperature of 40° to 50°F. They must also have full sunlight.

161. *I was given a little acacia plant that came along nicely during the summer. Why did it die when I transplanted it?*

Acacias are difficult to transplant because of the long tap root. If this suffers any damage, the plant is likely to die.

ACALYPHA

Two species of this Asiatic plant commonly grown. Chenille plant (*A. hispida*) has green foliage and long, fluffy, red flower tassels in winter. Firedragon plant (*A. wilkesiana*) has smaller winter flowers; leaves are mottled red, green, yellow, and brown

162. *Why does my acalypha growing in a southern window look wilted?*

Acalypha needs full sun and warmth but it also requires high humidity. Increase humidity and you should have no trouble (see 92).

163. *What soil is used for acalypha?*

This plant needs a porous mixture. Use equal parts loam, humus, and sand. Provide a good layer of drainage material in the bottom of the pot.

164. *Can I prevent my acalypha from getting so huge?*

If it is huge now, there is little you can do except to take cuttings and start new plants. They come along well if placed over mild heat. To prevent future plants from outgrowing your home, prune tops and roots about once a year in the spring. Return to the same pot but with fresh soil. Don't encourage a lot of growth by fertilizing and supplying successively larger pots.

ACANTHOSTACHYS STROBILACEA

Brazilian bromeliad with long, pendant, gray-green leaves, yellow spring flowers, and red conelike fruit—fine for hanging baskets

165. *I am tempted by the descriptions of acanthostachys, but can I grow it?*

Yes, this plant is handled like the other accommodating bromeliads. Primarily it needs sun and high humidity. See 342-353.

ACHIMENES

Rhizomatous tropical American gesneriads with velvety, gloxinialike flowers in purples, blues, reds, and white in summer

166. *What soil is used for achimenes and how much feeding is required?*

Use equal parts loam, humus, and sand and sterilize it (see 17). Feed every two weeks when in active growth. Some growers who plant the rhizomes in straight leaf mold (it should be coarse) find that plants do well with almost no fertilizer.

167. *When and how are achimenes planted?*

Plant January through March—five or six rhizomes to a standard 6-inch pot. Lay the rhizomes flat and cover with 1 inch of soil. Water just enough to keep the soil slightly moist. Grow at about 75°F until shoots are about 2 inches long.

168. *What causes pale foliage and poor growth on an achimenes growing in a south window?*

Achimenes do not like so much sun. Move them into an east window, where they will get sun only early in the morning but good light throughout the day. Warmth should be constant (65° to 75°F) during the growing season, and humidity fairly high.

169. *How can I make a sparse achimenes plant bush out?*

Pruning now may help, but in the future, to get a bushy plant, pinch out all the stems when they are 3 to 4 inches long.

170. *How are achimenes handled after they have bloomed?*

Gradually withhold water. Cut off foliage when soil is dry. Then either leave the rhizomes in the pot and store in a cool, dry place or lift them and store in sand or vermiculite. Divide rhizomes only in spring.

171. *If achimenes rhizomes sprout in storage, must they be planted immediately?*

If you do not water rhizomes that have sprouted, you can hold them in check without damage for several months.

172. *Can achimenes be propagated from the little waxy cones among the upper leaves?*

Yes. Gather these before they drop and store in dry sand or vermiculite until you want to plant them. You can also propagate achimenes by stem or leaf cuttings or by division of the rhizomes.

ACORUS GRAMINEUS VARIEGATUS

Small clump of green-and-white grasslike foliage

173. Is acorus an easy house plant?

Yes, if you have a room that doesn't go over 55°F. Grow in good light and give plenty of moisture because bogs and marshes are this plant's habitat.

AECHMEA

South American bromeliads with rosettes of handsome leaves, often colored, and clusters of yellow or red flowers sometimes tipped with blue in different seasons depending on species

174. What potting soil shall I use for an aechmea?

Use the standard bromeliad mixture (see 343).

175. What are the most favorable growing conditions for aechmea?

Plenty of water while making growth—keep the vase formed by the foliage filled. Good light at all times, but do not expose to summer sun. Average home temperature.

176. Why has my aechmea changed shape and color since I had it outdoors under the trees last summer?

The shade was probably too deep. When you move aechmea outdoors, place it in light shade like that provided by a tall maple or oak.

AESCHYNANTHUS (lipstick vine)

Also known as *Trichosporum.* Trailing tropical gesneriads with attractive leaves and scarlet or orange flowers in spring, summer, and fall

177. Why doesn't my aeschynanthus bloom? I am growing it with my African violets.

To prevent bud blast, aeschynanthus needs the same humidity as African violets; but to bloom well, it requires more sun.

178. What is the best temperature for aeschynanthus?

Between 70° and 80°F in the warm-weather flowering period. During the fall-winter rest period, a temperature around 60°F is better.

179. When should I prune aeschynanthus?

Flowers appear on ripe, mature wood, so don't prune until the fall, when flowering stops. At that time, let the plants rest a while by giving only a little water and no fertilizer.

AFRICAN VIOLET (*Saintpaulia*)

A gesneriad from Africa and the most popular of all house plants with nearly continuous flowers in purples, blues, whites, pinks, reds, bicolors, and multicolors

180. Do African violets require a special soil mixture?

No, many different porous, well-drained mixtures are used. If you mix your own soil, combine 1 part loam, 1 part sand or vermiculite, and 1 part humus. It's a good idea to add 1 part rotted manure. Or buy a convenient commercial mixture prepared especially for African violets and already sterilized.

181. Why must soil for African violets be sterilized?

To kill the nematodes and fungi that attack these plants. If you do not use a commercial sterilized potting soil formulated for African violets, sterilize the soil you mix yourself (see 17).

182. *What are the best containers for African violets?*

Use the type of clay, ceramic, or plastic pot you like best. Growers have success with all of these, although there has been trouble with clay pots because leaf stems resting on the rims often rot. This can be avoided (see 211). Scrub all containers thoroughly with soap and water before using them, and before reuse disinfect with boiling water and Clorox.

183. *What pot sizes are generally used for African violets?*

It depends on the size of the plant. To start a small plant, 2¼- or 2½-inch pots are large enough; 3's are adequate for plants with a spread of less than 8 inches; 4's are used for most big plants. Larger pots are rarely needed. Because the root system tends to be shallow, squatty pots such as bulb pans are preferred (see 31).

184. *Should African violets be repotted frequently?*

No. Unless they crowd pots with roots, they need repotting only about once a year—more often, perhaps, if they are still small fast growers. Type of soil, growing conditions, and age of plants all affect the rate of root formation. Use fresh sterilized soil when repotting and ruff up the roots a little to encourage growth.

185. *How often should African violets be watered?*

This depends on how dry your house is and how big the plants are. Water enough to keep the soil surface barely moist. Do not allow it to become really dry or actually soggy. Strive for the happy medium, and never let plants stand in water. Remove excess from saucers an hour or so after watering.

186. *Is it true that African violets must be watered only from the bottom?*

No. People who insist on bottom watering do so because they find this more convenient or have heard that water on the leaves does damage. It is true that if you get *cold* water on foliage, unsightly spots may develop; and if sun shines on wet foliage, burning may result. But you can avoid these problems by using tepid water, getting as little as possible on the leaves and not exposing them to the sun. In other words, if it is more convenient for you to water from overhead, go ahead. But remember that whichever way you usually water African violets, you should *occasionally* do it the other way, too (see 188).

187. *How long should I let pots of African violets stand in water when they need moisture?*

Only until the soil feels quite damp on top. Do not let pots stand in water for hours. Waterlogging prevents proper aeration of soil.

188. *I have always watered African violets from below, but a friend told me I should sometimes water from the top, too. Is this true?*

Occasional watering from the top helps to distribute fertilizer evenly through the soil and flushes down fertilizer salts which tend to accumulate on the soil surface and the rims of the pots when bottom-watering alone is practiced. Conversely, if you water regularly from the top, you should occasionally water from the bottom just to make sure that the soil is uniformly moist.

189. *What fertilizer should I use for African violets and how often?*

Any commercial fertilizer that has twice as much phosphorus as nitrogen and potassium is good. This might be a 5-10-5 dry fertilizer or a 15-30-15 liquid fertilizer. There are also many excellent products made just for African violets. In all cases, follow the manufacturer's directions for use.

190. *How often should African violets be fertilized?*

Fertilize African violets about every two to three weeks through the year. Make applications when soil is damp.

191. *What causes the foliage of my African violets to get yellow and to stop growing?*

You are probably giving them too much fertilizer. Follow the directions of the manufacturer as to amounts. Other possible causes of yellowing are too much sun, too dry air, too much or too little watering, too small a pot, too deep planting.

192. *Do African violets require high humidity?*

Yes, and they will not thrive without it. A relative humidity of 70 to 80 per cent is desirable but not common in homes. To create enough, place pots on ½-inch layers of pebbles in pots or saucers, and keep a level of water in either container just below the base of the pots. Spraying foliage frequently—daily if possible—with a fine mist of lukewarm water is also desirable, but do not expose plants to sunlight until foliage dries. Running a water-filled coffee percolator in the room also helps.

193. *What is the most desirable temperature for African violets?*

During the day, 65° to 75°F; at night, 60° to 65°F. Don't let the temperature fall below 60°F or go beyond 75°F; otherwise, growth and bloom will both be poor.

194. *Is it safe to keep African violets in a well-ventilated bedroom?*

It is if they are not exposed to too low temperatures or cold drafts. African violets need fresh air.

195. *Why don't my African violets in an east window grow and bloom well?*

When light is good, as here, and plants still don't bloom, there is always the possibility of too little humidity, too high heat, or a chill from nearness to the glass in very cold weather. However, causes of non-blooming can be quite complex. These are just three possibilities.

196. *Will African violets bloom in a north window?*

Yes, if the location is fully light and open, though not as well as in an east window. Through the hot summer months, a north window is ideal.

197. *How much sun can African violets take?*

More than most people seem to think. They do best in an east or west window or a south window lightly curtained at midday and in early afternoon. The reaction of the plants to their exposure is your best guide. If foliage does not burn and bloom is good, there isn't too much sun. On the other hand, if stems become too long, foliage is pale and soft, and bloom is sparse, there isn't enough sun.

198. *My African violets are in an east window that gets sun for about an hour and a half a day in winter; but the bloom is sparse. Do they need more sun?*

Probably they do. Move them into another east or west window where they will get more hours of sun; or put them in a south window for a while (see 197). An old saying about African violets is that "more light will bring a shy bloomer into flower."

199. *How much fluorescent light should I provide for African violets?*

Use a fixture with two or more 48-inch fluorescent tubes. The rims of the pots should be about 12 inches below the lights, but you can vary this spacing up or down a few inches according to the size and response of the plants.

200. *If I grow African violets entirely under electric light, how long should they be exposed to the light each day?*

Fourteen to fifteen hours.

201. *How do I clean African violet foliage?*

Brush off the leaves occasionally with a soft paint brush or the furry side of an extra leaf. Spray with lukewarm water once a month, and let foliage dry before exposure to sun. (*Illustration 12*)

12. Cleaning African violet leaves

202. *Do African violets need a rest period?*

No, as long as you give them good care, they go right on blooming the year round. But if you want the largest possible flowers in winter, it is wise not to push them too hard in summer. Slack off watering and feeding a trifle, and remove some of the flowers and buds.

203. *Should African violets be summered outdoors in the garden?*

No, the hazards of wind, rain, and sun are too great, and in many places summer heat and humidity are high enough to be harmful. A screened porch is good if it does not get too hot.

204. *How can I take care of my African violets when I go on vacation?*

Let a trusted neighbor watch over them if possible. Otherwise, try one of these ideas that others have used successfully for up to two weeks: (1) Water plants the day before you leave. Remove old leaves, buds, and flowers. The day you leave, cover plants with polyethylene film arranged in a tent so that it does not touch the foliage. (2) Put a layer of wet sphagnum moss in a carton or wash boiler. Remove old leaves, buds, and flowers, and water plants well. Then set plants on the moss and screen them from sun in order to retard evaporation.

205. *How do I propagate an African violet that has developed a second crown?*

Remove it from the pot and cut the crowns apart with a sharp knife. Gently separate the roots. Then replant separately and usually in two smaller pots. To avoid breaking too many leaves while performing this operation, first let the soil dry out more than usual. The leaves will then be more resistant to damage.

206. *What are the best ways to propagate African violets?*

These are all good: (1) Cut off a vigorous, mature (but not too old) leaf with a 1½-inch stem. Insert the stem through a hole in cardboard and place over a tumbler of water with the stem end about 1 inch in the water. (2) Insert 1 inch of the leaf stem in wet sand and cover with polyethylene film or a jelly jar. When roots develop, pot up the plantlets in prepared African violet soil in 2-inch pots. If the original big leaf is severed from the little plant, it can often be propagated again. (3) Divide a multiple-crowned plant by letting it dry out a little, then remove it from the pot and gently pull or cut it into sections (see 143).

207. *Is it easy to raise African violets from seed?*

Yes, but not quite so easy as propagating in other ways (see 206). Sow the dust-fine seeds thinly in a flat or shallow pot filled with screened sphagnum moss or vermiculite. Set in water until the surface is just damp, then cover with glass or plastic film and keep in a warm place in good light, but not in sun. Do not overwater. When leaves appear, feed every two weeks with dilute fertilizer. Transplant into pots of sterile African violet soil (see 180) when seedlings have four leaves.

208. *What causes the center leaves of African violets to become twisted, shiny, and brittle?*

Cyclamen mites. If you spray with malathion, you can stop a mild infestation for a while. But for treatment that will last several months, set the pots in a dilute solution of sodium selenate until it soaks up through the soil (see 110). Discard badly infested plants and thereafter make it a practice to use an insecticide about once a month. NNOR, Optox spray, Antrol bomb, or Sel-Kaps are good preventives.

209. *One of my African violets has stopped growing and the plant is loose in the soil. The leaves are soft, yellowish, and turned down at the edges. What is the trouble?*

Nematodes—microscopic soil insects—cause this fairly common problem. You can confirm their presence by taking the plant out of the pot and examining the roots for small knots or lumps. There is no effective cure. Destroy the plant. In the future, treat plants with VC-13 as a preventive.

210. *Why should an African violet plant become floppy and limp, with rotting main stems?*

The trouble is crown rot. Destroy the plant but save healthy leaves for propagation.

211. *My African violets are in red clay pots. How can I prevent rotting of leaf-stems where they touch pot rims?*

Petiole or leaf-stem rot is not serious but is disfiguring. It is caused by contact with an accumulation of mineral salts on pot rims. To prevent trouble, cover pot rims with strips of aluminum foil or cellulose tape, or dip rims in melted paraffin. Water often enough from the top to wash the soluble salts down into the soil away from the surface and the pot rims.

AGAVE

A large genus of tropical American succulents—including the century plant—many low-growing, with sword-shaped leaves in a rosette, and greenish-yellow flowers in spring and summer

212. *What is good culture for agaves?*

For soil, a mixture of 2 parts loam, 1 part leaf mold, and 1 part sand. They require a great deal of sun and air and should therefore be grown outdoors for as many months as possible. Watering should be somewhat heavier than for other succulents.

213. *Why doesn't my century plant bloom?*

Agaves do not bloom until they are very old. That is the reason for the name "century plant."

214. *How are agaves propagated?*

Primarily by offshoots, which they produce abundantly. Also by seed (see 965). And some agaves produce bulbils above ground. These can also be propagated. Just detach and plant them in sand.

ALLAMANDA CATHARTICA HENDERSONI (golden trumpet)

Large climber from South America with big, yellow, funnel-shaped flowers in summer

215. *Is allamanda a good house plant?*

It is if you have the space for it. It grows rapidly in warm weather to as tall as 40 feet, and unless you prune new shoots at the end of winter, it may become leggy and overcrowd your space.

216. *What does allamanda require in the way of sun and water?*

Full sun. Lots of water while growing and fertilizer every couple of weeks. To climb, the stems need to be tied to wires or some other support.

ALOCASIA

Genus of tropical Asiatic plants with large, roughly triangular leaves often in variegated colors

217. *How much light should an alocasia be given?*

Alocasia thrives at an east window. It cannot stand too much sun. In the summer, when you put it outdoors, it should be grown in light shade.

218. *What causes my alocasia to drop its leaves and look almost dead?*

Either the temperature or the humidity is too low. Alocasias come from the tropics and therefore require a temperature not lower than 65°F and plenty of humidity.

219. *Can I start new plants from the suckers my alocasia sent up in summer?*

Cut off the suckers, each with a bit of root, and plant in a peat moss-sand mixture until they are growing well. Then pot them in African violet soil (see 180).

ALOE

Large genus of rugged, decorative, mostly African succulents with toothed or spiny leaves, usually in rosettes, and cylindrical red or yellow flower clusters in fall and winter

220. *How are aloes cultivated?*

See 957-965. If kept fairly dry, aloes can stand very low temperatures but not frost.

221. *Why do stem-cuttings of aloes rot?*

Cutting the stems of some types often starts rot. Try

pressing the cut end of the stem with a hot iron before inserting it in the rooting medium.

ALPINIA

Tall, slender, tropical Asiatic plants with long leaves and multi-colored, orchidlike, summer flowers in some varieties

222. *Is alpinia really a greenhouse plant?*

It does better under greenhouse conditions but can be grown in the house if you provide high enough humidity. Grow at 65° to 75°F.

223. *What soil and light does alpinia require? What about watering?*

Use general-purpose soil (see 1). Grow in good light but avoid much sun. An east window is fine. Keep soil moist but not wet.

AMARYLLIS (*Hippeastrum*)

Tall, tropical, bulbous plant with huge lilylike flowers in white, red, pink and multicolors in winter and spring

224. *Is an amaryllis bulb selling for $6.00 worth so much more than one selling for $1.00?*

Prices are based on size of bulbs and the newness and availability of varieties. Both the $1.00 and $6.00 bulbs will produce handsome flowers. But as a general rule, the more expensive (and larger) the bulb, the larger and more numerous the flowers produced.

225. *How is an amaryllis bulb potted?*

Select a pot 2 inches larger in diameter than the bulb. Set the bulb so that about half of it extends above the general-purpose soil (see 1). Insert a 2-foot stake in the soil when you plant the bulb. Keep the pot in a warm, shaded spot and water sparingly until growth begins. Then move into sunlight and increase the water supply as it is needed. (*Illustration 13*)

13. How an amaryllis is potted

226. *Can I speed up the blooming of an amaryllis?*

Flowering normally starts six to eight weeks after the bulb is planted. You can gain a week or two if you place the pot on top of three or four magazines on a warm radiator only until the flower bud emerges.

227. *I've been disappointed in the length of time my amaryllis flowers last. How can I make them stay fresh for a longer period?*

If you keep the plant fairly cool (at 65°F, say) as the flowers appear, they will last longer. Prior to blooming, plants tolerate 60° to 75°F, but they should not be grown next to a cold window.

228. *How do you handle amaryllis bulbs after they have bloomed?*

After flowers fade, cut off the bloom stalks 2 inches above the bulb, but keep the leaves growing through the summer so the bulbs can store up enough nourishment to bloom again the next year. To promote this plant growth, keep the soil damp and apply a little liquid fertilizer once a month.

229. *Should amaryllis bulbs be moved outdoors in summer?*

Many people do this to get the big plants out of the house. It is a convenience, not a necessity. You can move them outdoors after danger of frost has passed. Sink the pots to within 1 inch of the soil surface in a semishaded part of the garden and stand them on a thick layer of hard cinders or gravel so soil will not become waterlogged and worms will not tunnel in. Water regularly (do not depend on rain) and fertilize once a month. Stake the leaves. Before the first fall frost, lift the pots and bring indoors.

230. *What do I do in the fall with an amaryllis I have kept growing through the summer?*

Whether you keep bulbs indoors or out, in early fall, stop watering entirely and let the leaves turn yellow. If they do not wither and fall off by November 1, cut them off 1 to 2 inches above the bulb. Then store the bulb, still in its pot, in a cool (about 55°F), dark place. Apply a little water about once a month to keep roots from drying out. After a couple of months —usually about January 1—the bulb will be ready to grow again.

231. *Are amaryllis easily propagated?*

In time, bulbs naturally produce bulblets, which can be

separated when well developed and grown separately in pots. Or you can grow amaryllis from seed. Professionals also reproduce plants by division of the bulbs, but the process is tricky and the results far from certain.

232. *Is it possible to grow amaryllis in water like hyacinths?*

Yes, place the bulb in a hyacinth glass or in pebbles with water just up to the base. Grow in a shady place until buds appear and then move into sunlight. Support the growing plant so that the heavy foliage and flowers do not tip over. Don't try to save a water-grown bulb.

AMAZON LILY (*Eucharis grandiflora*)

South American bulbous plant with fragrant white blooms on long stems in winter and again in spring

233. *Don't I need a greenhouse to grow an Amazon lily plant?*

Not if you can give the plant a house temperature of 65° to 75°F, high humidity, and an east window. It grows in general-purpose soil (see 1) with a double amount of humus. Water generously during active growth.

234. *How can I get my eucharis lily to bloom twice a year?*

After the first flowering, withhold water until the leaves begin to wilt, then water thoroughly, then let dry again, then water thoroughly, and so on. Keep this up for a month, then give a thorough soaking, and hope for the best. Not every one succeeds in getting repeat bloom from this plant.

235. *How are Amazon lilies propagated?*

By natural division of the bulbs. But do not actually separate them until the clump has developed to large size. Eucharis resents frequent disturbance.

AMONUM CARDAMON

Large East Indian plant with long, broad, spicy leaves

236. *How much sun should I give a plant of amonum?*

It can take an eastern or western exposure, but really likes little sun and therefore does well at a north window.

237. *Is amonum cardamon a moisture-loving plant?*

When it is making growth, yes. Give enough water to keep the general-purpose soil (see 1) moist at all times. When the plant starts to rest in fall, very little water is required. In fact, some people let the soil dry out completely.

ANEMONE CORONARIA (poppy anemone)

Tuberous-rooted Mediterranean plant bearing delightful long-stemmed, poppylike flowers in red, blue, and white from October through the winter

238. *Are anemones easily grown indoors?*

Not unless you can provide the very low (40°F) night temperature they require. Their culture is similar to that of ranunculus (see 884-888).

ANNUAL FLOWERS

These questions deal with annuals in general; specific information is given for browallia and morning glories

239. *Which annuals are most easily grown indoors?*

Alyssum, browallia, balsam, forget-me-nots, lobelia, some marigolds, morning glories, nicotiana, and snapdragons.

240. *How and when are annuals started for indoor use?*

It is best to sow seeds outdoors in summer and bring in

the small plants before frost. Or you can take cuttings from plants growing outdoors and bring them in after they have rooted.

241. *Why aren't the annuals that I potted to grow indoors blooming?*

Annuals need a great deal of sun and temperatures somewhat lower than normal in the home. Marigolds and snapdragons, for instance, thrive at 65°F; forget-me-nots, at 50°F.

APHELANDRA SQUARROSA LOUISAE

Erect tropical American shrub with shiny green, white-veined leaves and yellow flower spikes in summer

242. *My neighbor gets two blooming periods from aphelandra but I get only one. What can I do to get better results?*

Just give your plant good culture. This one needs extra humus in the soil and a temperature of about 70°F. Keep the soil moist but not wet. Grow in good light—an east window or south window lightly shaded at midday during the summer. After the plant has bloomed, let it rest fairly dry for about a month.

243. *How can the legginess of an aphelandra plant be controlled?*

This is difficult because legginess is a natural tendency. Pinch out young growth and start new plants from cuttings every year rather than try to cope with an old specimen.

APOSTLE PLANT (*Neomarica*)

Also called twelve apostles plant. Brazilian, 2-foot, rhizomatous plant resembling iris, with twelve sword-shaped leaves in a fan and large, fragrant, late winter flowers, white with violet markings

244. *What is the proper culture for the apostle plant?*

A general-purpose soil (see 1) and a tight fitting pot. Good light during growth and sunlight when blooming. Regular watering. Temperature of 70°F.

245. *Where can I obtain an apostle plant? None of the florists or garden stores here carry it.*

Though it is a common enough house plant, it is difficult to buy. Better ask a friend who has one to share it with you. The plant is propagated by division of the rhizome after flowering. Or you can remove the little plants that form on some of the stalks after flowering. They will bloom in about two years.

246. *How can I keep the tips of apostle plant leaves from yellowing?*

It will help to spray frequently with water or hold the plant right under a running faucet. Such deterioration of foliage is almost always the result of too little humidity.

ARALIA (*Dizygotheca*)

Large foliage plant from the Pacific with graceful, often drooping leaves of varying form

247. *Why have the leaves of my aralia shriveled?*

Probably because the air is too dry. The commonly grown aralia requires moist soil and high humidity. Spray the foliage regularly and increase humidity any other way you can (see 92). Keep the plant away from direct sun.

248. *Can I save an aralia that has lost its leaves?*

Cut it down close to the soil in the spring and put it outdoors in filtered shade. Keep watered and fertilized and spray the foliage with water. It should come back. But if you are particularly attached to this plant, it would be well also to propagate some of the stems you cut off.

ARDISIA CRISPA (coral berry)

Also identified as *Ardisia crenulata.* Compact tropical Asiatic shrub with shiny, wavy-margined leaves and clusters of red berries at Christmas

249. *Is it true that an ardisia should be grown in a cool room?*

Yes, at about 60°F it will thrive in a north window in winter and hold its summer-ripened berries. Move it outdoors into light shade for the summer.

250. *Can an ardisia be grown from the seeds in the fruits?*

Yes. Remove the pulp, sow the seeds in the spring and then wait. It may take six months for germination. You can also propagate by cuttings of young stems that have almost matured. And you can air-layer plants that have become leggy (see 141).

ASPARAGUS

Feathery-foliaged plants mainly from Africa, some of which resemble ferns, that climb or trail. Two of the best species for the house are *A. plumosus* and *A. sprengeri*

251. *What are the requirements of asparagus ferns?*

Give plenty of water and fertilize *A. sprengeri* every two weeks during the growing period. Spray the foliage with water once a week to keep down red spider, a common pest. Grow in an east or west window at about 55° to 60°F.

252. *How can asparagus be trained as a vine?*

A. plumosus, the plumy asparagus that florists add to bouquets, climbs naturally on string or a trellis. *A. sprengeri,* considered the better species for indoor culture, is a trailing, needled plant but it can also be encouraged to climb on string.

253. *How is asparagus propagated?*

The easiest way is from seed. Soak seed overnight before sowing in a flat or pot of sandy soil. Keep in the dark until growth starts.

ASPIDISTRA (cast-iron plant)

Large Chinese plant with long, heavy, glossy leaves. It grows under even the worst conditions

254. *Why is aspidistra called the cast-iron plant?*

Because it withstands so much abuse. It needs little light; is not particular about temperature; is hardly affected by smoke, dust, or manufactured gas fumes; and endures considerable neglect. But it does better if regularly watered and occasionally sprayed or sponged with water to keep foliage clean.

255. *Why has my aspidistra lost the white stripes in its leaves?*

The striped leaves of *Aspidistra elatior variegata* may change to solid green if the soil is too rich or is not well drained.

256. *How do I propagate an aspidistra?*

Divide roots in the spring and pot the sections in 4-inch pots in general-purpose soil (see 1).

AUSTRALIAN SILK OAK (*Grevillea robusta*)

A large tree that grows indoors to about 3 feet, with feathery, fernlike leaves

257. *What care does a silk oak require?*

Give it a well-drained, general-purpose soil (see 1), kept damp but not soaking; good light but only a few hours of sun; a temperature of about 50° to 60°F.

258. *Why doesn't my Australian silk oak flower?*

Grown outdoors, silk oak bears orange flowers and develops into a tree 100 feet high or more. But indoors it is a smallish shrub that rarely blooms.

259. *What are my chances of growing a silk oak from seed?*

Excellent. There is no trick to it and you should have a large plant within a year (see 144).

AVOCADO (*Persea americana*)

Familiar tropical fruit tree grown indoors for its foliage

260. *Is it better to plant an avocado seed in soil or in water?*

Soil is better. Use a general-purpose mixture (see 1). Plant the seed, large end down, ½ inch below the surface of the soil in a 4-inch pot.

261. *I haven't succeeded in starting an avocado seed in water. How is it done?*

Seeds started in water sometimes decay. Stick three toothpicks into the sides of the seed and suspend it in a tumbler so that the base just touches the water. When roots develop, pot in soil and grow in good light.

262. *Why doesn't my avocado bear fruit? It must be fifteen years old and is 7 feet high.*

Your avocado will not bear fruit unless another avocado of a different variety is grown nearby to fertilize the flowers. It is not self-fertile.

AZALEA

Familiar, beautiful, spring-flowering shrub in many colors, from North America and Asia

263. *Why did the azalea I was given at Easter lose all its leaves after blooming?*

It may have become infested with red spider or perhaps you did not water it enough. Before, during, and after flowering, azaleas need quantities of water. They also need good light and a cool (50° to 60°F) room.

264. *Can I save an azalea that lost its leaves after flowering?*

It is unlikely, but you might try. Cut back the tops half way and give the culture outlined in 263. If no new leaves come out on the pruned top in a couple of weeks, you may as well throw the plant away.

265. *Should the azalea I was given be planted outdoors in the spring?*

Yes, and if you intend to bring it in again in the fall, keep it in its pot and plunge it in a lightly shaded spot in the garden. Keep well watered during the summer and spray the leaves with water to ward off red spider. Prune back shoots that grow too long. If this is a hardy type, you can plant it permanently outdoors.

266. *Can I bring my gift azalea of last year into bloom again this coming winter?*

You can with considerable effort. Keep the plant outdoors during the summer (see 265). Before hard frost, bring it indoors and store in a cool (40° to 50°F), light place. Water just enough to keep the soil from drying out completely. In January or early February, move the plant to a sunny window in a somewhat warmer (60°F) room and increase watering. Feed with a balanced fertilizer. Bloom should start in about five weeks. The keys to success are cool growing and water.

267. *Can azaleas grown for indoor use be permanently planted outdoors?*

In temperate climates, where you see them growing as garden plants, most gift azaleas can safely be planted out in spring. But in very cold climates, they may be winterkilled.

268. *What soil do azaleas require?*

Equal parts loam, sand, and peat moss with the addition of oak leaf mold. To maintain the acidity that azaleas require, work into the soil 1 teaspoonful of ammonium sulfate once a month during the summer and water it in well.

269. *When should an azalea be repotted?*

In the spring after blooming, but only if it is too large for the pot. If possible, shake off some of the old soil and repot the plant in the same container with a fresh mixture of acid soil worked in around the roots. Otherwise, use a pot just one size larger.

270. *Can I propagate azaleas from stem cuttings?*

The small-flowered Kurume azaleas can often be propagated from the short stems that develop after blooming.

BABYS-TEARS (*Helxine solieroli*)

Also called Irish moss or Corsican carpet plant, a creeper from Corsica and Sardinia with tiny mosslike leaves

271. How much light does babys-tears require?

A bright light but little, if any, sun. Grow it in a north window or a not-too-sunny east window. Keep the general-purpose soil mixture (see 1) damp. You can even let the pot stand in a saucer of water.

272. How can I propagate babys-tears?

Just cut out a small section of a growing plant, press it into soil, and keep well watered. Although it may seem to start slowly, it will soon take hold and spread fast.

BASKET GRASS (*Oplismenus compositus*)

Also identified as *O. hirtellus,* a sprawling, tropical grass with wide, 4-inch-long, pink-, white-, and green-striped leaves

273. What is the best way to propagate basket grass?

Either divide the roots or start stem cuttings in moist sand or water (they root at the joints). This is an easy-to-multiply plant and also easy to grow if it has warmth, some humidity, some sun (as at an east window), and regular watering.

BEGONIA

Favorite winter- and spring-flowering tropical plants with white, pink, and red flowers. Favorite types discussed here are the wax (semperflorens), calla lily, angel wing, hairy-leaved, basket, beefsteak, rex, Christmas, and tuberous begonias

274. What is a good soil for begonias?

One that is light, porous, moisture-retentive. For all but the rhizomatous begonias, mix 2 parts loam, 2 parts humus, and 1 part sand. For rhizomatous types, such as beefsteak and rex begonias, use equal parts loam, humus, and sand.

275. *Do begonias have any preference for certain types of containers?*

You can plant them in anything but, because they are shallow-rooted, it is unnecessary to use a standard (deep) pot. A bulb or azalea pot is better.

276. *When should begonias be repotted?*

When they stop growing or when roots come out through the drainage hole of the pot or when the outside of the root-ball is completely covered with roots. When you do repot, break the root-ball slightly apart so that the roots will grow outward. Do not pack in the new soil too tight.

277. *How often should begonias be fertilized and with what?*

Use any balanced commercial fertilizer and apply it about every two to three weeks from the time plants start into growth until they stop flowering. During their rest period after flowering, plants do not need to be fed.

278. *How often should I water begonias?*

When soil surface is dry to the touch. Then, when you do water, make sure the soil is wet all the way through. Avoid overwatering begonias or letting them stand in water.

279. *Does hard water hurt begonias?*

Very hard water is bad. So is very soft water. Rain water is the ideal for begonias and all other house plants.

280. *What is the best temperature for begonias?*

Generally, they do well in a day temperature of 65° to 75°F and 60° to 65°F at night.

281. *Will begonias do well in a north window?*

If it is fully light, they will grow but bloom very little, if at all. Keep them in an east or west window. They will even be all right in a south window if shielded from the midday sun in late winter, spring, and summer.

282. *Do begonias grow well under fluorescent light?*

Begonias thrive under fluorescents. The wax begonias can be placed within 8 inches of the lights; the rex type, about 14 inches; others, in between. Give them fourteen to sixteen hours of light a day (either all fluorescent or part fluorescent and part natural daylight).

283. *Why do the leaves of my begonia get crisp and dry at the edges and then fall?*

Probably the atmosphere is too dry. In general, begonias need fairly high humidity. Place the pots in pebble-filled saucers (see 92) or take the plants to the sink and spray them daily with water.

284. *What can I do about a favorite begonia that has grown leggy?*

When the plants start to grow actively in the spring, cut out the old stems. Then, when the young new stems are several inches tall, pinch off the growing tips.

285. *Should begonias go outdoors in the summer?*

Yes, after all danger of frost is past. They will develop

well in open air. Plunge pots up to the rims in soil in a partially shaded and protected place. Put a layer of gravel or hard cinders under pots. Or set plants on the porch in the light but out of the wind.

286. *What causes the deformed buds and flowers on my begonias?*

Possibly cyclamen mites; possibly thrips. In either case, spray with a miticide such as malathion. A dry atmosphere also causes new buds to dry up.

287. *What ails one of my begonias that is slowly dying and has funny looking bumps on the stem?*

Root knot. Don't try to save the plant. In the future, use only sterilized soil (see 17).

288. *What is causing the leaves of some of my begonias to turn a shiny rust color?*

Leaf nematodes, which are very difficult to control and may spread. Destroy the plants. In the future, sterilize soil for begonias (see 17).

289. *How can I get rid of the grayish mold on the leaves of one of my begonias?*

This is probably botrytis, a fungus that spreads rapidly when plants are grown in poor light with too high humidity and not enough ventilation. Better destroy the plant before the fungus spreads to others. If you want to try to save the plant, isolate it, cut out all infected parts, and treat cut surfaces with fermate.

290. *How are begonias grown from seed?*

Sow the seed in very fine, light, sterile, moist soil or finely ground sphagnum moss, and place pot or flat in dim light in a cool (about 65°F) place. Bottom heat will speed germination. When growth appears, move into good light (but not sun) and to a warmer place. Cover loosely with polyethylene film to maintain humidity. When plants develop three leaves, transplant to a flat of sterile soil. Grow there until seedlings become crowded. Then shift to individual pots and give weekly applications of very dilute fertilizer. Wax begonia seeds can be sown at any time; other indoor species are best sown in early spring.

291. *What are the best growing conditions for wax begonias?*

These plump, free-branching begonias with rounded, crisp, waxy leaves and a habit of almost continuous flowering thrive in east or west windows in a temperature no higher than 70°F. Water only when the soil feels quite dry, but not on dark days. Fertilize monthly except right after flowering. Best growth and flowering occur when roots are pot-bound. Wax begonias are among the most satisfactory of flowering house plants.

292. *Why do some of my wax begonias get leggy and fail to branch?*

This type of begonia needs to be pinched back when small—about 5 inches tall; and it may need regular pinching back as it grows to encourage side shoots to form. Turn plants regularly so that all sides are exposed to full light. A cooler room and less water discourage leggy growth.

293. *I was told that wax begonias do not like as much humidity as other types. Why, then, should my "rosebuds" be doing poorly?*

The double-flowered wax begonias, such as the rosebud

and camellia types, actually need more humidity than others in this group, but all begonias require a fair amount of humidity.

294. *Should an old wax begonia be cut back?*

Yes. If it has become scraggly, cut back the old stems right to the soil after flowering slows down. The plant will renew itself, especially if you repot in fresh soil at the time of cutting back. The cut stems can be rooted in water or a sand-peat moss mixture if you want new plants.

295. *How are wax begonias propagated?*

By putting stem cuttings in a jar of water or inserting them in a moist mixture of sand and peat moss. Do not cover them to hold in moisture because they may rot. The best cuttings are those taken from the base of the plant, not from the tips; and to ensure that they will develop into bushy plants, the cuttings should include a branch.

296. *What is the secret of success with the calla lily begonias?*

Calla lily begonias are a type of wax begonia distinguished by young leaves that are white and shaped like calla lilies. In general, treat them like other wax begonias but grow them cooler—not above 65°F with a night temperature somewhat lower. They also need even more humidity and somewhat less sun. Protect from drafts. And once you have set the plants in an east window, leave them there; they should not be shifted around though of course they should be turned at the window to prevent one-sided growth.

297. *Why have I failed to root stem cuttings of calla lily begonias?*

If the leaves on the cuttings were all or almost all white,

that explains your problem. Half of the leaf area or more should be green. Unlike other wax begonias, calla lily begonias also need to be rooted in a humid atmosphere, such as is provided by a covering of polyethylene film.

298. *Do angel wing begonias require special care?*

No. These begonias with leaves shaped like angel wings and usually with bamboolike stems and winter and spring flowers are easy to grow. Just follow the general rules (see 274-285). Overwatering is the greatest hazard: let the soil dry out completely before each thorough soaking, and don't let water stand in the saucers. Prune plants fairly regularly to keep them from getting too tall.

299. *Are angel wing begonias propagated like other types?*

Yes. Place stem cuttings in water or in a mixture of sand and peat moss (see 130-133), or divide the plants at the roots.

300. *How are hairy-leaved begonias grown and propagated?*

See general rules (274-285) for the culture of begonias with hairy leaves and fuzzy flowers at different times of the year, depending on variety. Propagate by planting stem cuttings in a medium of 2 parts sand and 1 part peat moss. Cover the flat or pot with polyethylene film, but remove it often so that humidity does not become too high and bring on rot.

301. *Why should some of my basket begonias do so poorly when others right alongside do so well?*

Probably because they are different species. Many types of begonias can be grown in baskets, but each requires the special care generally given for the species.

302. *How can I make my basket begonia fill out?*

Pinch out the growing tips of the stems. New branches will then develop.

303. *Can basket begonias be propagated by layering?*

This is a good method. Pin down a stem, at the third-from-the-top joint, onto soil in an adjacent pot. When roots form, cut off the stem below them and pot the new plant in standard begonia soil.

304. *Are beefsteak begonias tricky to grow successfully?*

The popular beefsteak begonia with its round leaves, red underneath, and spring flowers is one of a large group of rhizomatous types. Avoid overwatering and overfertilizing. Spray foliage with water as often as possible. Give full sun in winter and supplement it, especially on gray days, with artificial light. When plants go dormant in fall, stop fertilizing and water sparingly.

305. *How are beefsteak begonias planted?*

Use a shallow container such as a bulb pan filled with equal parts loam, humus, and sand. Lay the rhizome on top of the soil with the growing tip as far in from the pot rim as possible. Water just enough to moisten the soil all the way through. All rhizomatous begonias are planted like this.

306. *What are the best ways to propagate rhizomatous begonias like the beefsteak?*

By leaf cuttings or cuttings from the tips of the rhizomes. Leaves should have 2-inch stems and be stuck into moist sand at an angle. With rhizomes, take off one of the pointed ends so that the cutting has an eye, top and bottom. Dust the cut surface with sulfur. (Dust the cut on the old rhizome, too.) Remove the larger leaves and insert the rhizome cutting in a mixture of sand and peat moss. Cuttings from plants with horizontal rhizomes are laid flat, half in and half out of the soil. Cuttings from plants with vertical rhizomes are set upright with the base ½ inch in the soil. Cover pot or flat with polyethylene film to maintain humidity, but keep the soil itself barely damp.

307. *Are rex begonias difficult to raise?*

In the average house, yes, but try them anyway. Their large, beautifully textured, many-colored leaves are worth the effort. Grow them in a temperature of 70° to 72°F. Maintain as high a humidity as possible (see 92) and keep the soil moist (see 309). Grow in a northeast window, where they will get full light but little sun.

308. *Do rex begonias have special potting requirements?*

Use standard begonia soil (see 274) with an extra amount of humus. Do not pack the soil tight around the rhizomes. Use small pots if you want to hold down the size of the plants.

309. *Why did my rex begonia drop all its leaves last fall?*

Rex begonias have a definite period of dormancy in late fall and winter. Different varieties react in different ways: some stop growing; some look peaked; some drop their leaves. If you are worried about your plant, check whether the rhizome is plump. If it is, it will start into growth again about February. Just keep it in a warm (about 65°F) place and water only occasionally.

310. *How are rex begonias propagated?*

In general, from leaf cuttings. These are made in three ways. (1) Take a leaf with 2 inches of stem and place the stem in a glass of water or insert it in moist sand. When growth develops where stem and leaf join, pot in soil so that the new growth rests on the surface. (2) Cut a leaf into triangular pieces, each with part of a main vein running down the center to the point of the triangle. Insert the points of each piece ½ inch deep in moist sand at an angle. (*Illustration 14*) (3) Take

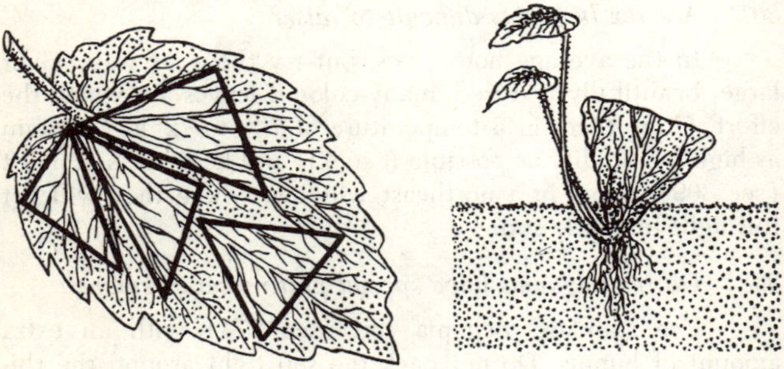

14. How to propagate rex begonias from leaf pieces

a leaf with a short piece of stem. Make small cuts across the back over the main veins. Insert the stem in moist sand so that the leaf rests, cut-side down, on the sand. Weight or pin it down. New plants will develop at the cuts. (*Illustration 15*)

311. How can I prolong the bloom of a Christmas begonia?

Place your Christmas or Melior begonia, a tuberous type, in an east window with as much humidity as you can provide and in heat not above 70°F. Keep the soil moist, but don't let pots stand in water and be careful not to let puddles stand in the leaves if you water from above. Admit fresh air daily but do not expose to chill drafts. In cold weather, let in fresh air from an adjoining room.

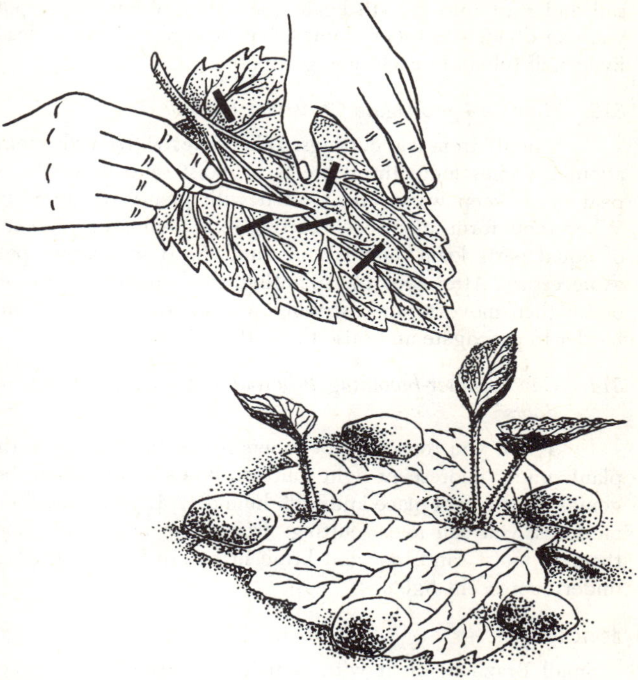

15. How to propagate rex begonias by cutting leaf veins

312. *Can Christmas begonias be carried over for another season?*

This isn't easy but perhaps worth a try. When blooming stops, cut back tops and put the plant in a cool (50° to 60°F) place. Water only enough to keep the soil from drying out. Rest the plant in this way for about two months. Then repot in fresh soil and start into growth again (see 311). When you repot, you can divide the tuber clumps; but be sure to leave at least five small tubers in each new group.

313. How do I propagate Christmas begonias?

Usually from leaf cuttings. Take leaves with sturdy stems about 2 inches long. Insert stems in moist sand or sand and peat moss, keep warm and shaded with plenty of humidity. When roots form, plant each cutting in a 2¼-inch pot in a soil of equal parts loam, humus, and sand. Shift into larger pots as necessary. After each transplanting, shade plants for a week or so; then move to an east window. Christmas begonias are harder to propagate and raise than other kinds.

314. Can summer-blooming tuberous begonias be grown indoors?

Yes, if you root and pot tubers in the fall and grow the plants under fluorescent light fourteen hours a day. These begonias need a cool place and high humidity. If you grow them outdoors, you can make cuttings from them in August. Root them in moist sand, pot and bring in before frost, and place under fluorescent lights.

BERTOLONIA

Small Brazilian plant with oval leaves attractively marked with purple or dark red

315. How is bertolonia grown indoors?

Pot in general-purpose soil (see 1) with a double amount of humus. Give plenty of moisture and fairly high humidity. Grow at 70°F in good light but with little sun—in an east window, for instance.

BILLBERGIA NUTANS (queens-tears)

Brazilian bromeliad with slender leaves growing in the form of a pineapple and green-and-yellow flowers hanging from pink bracts in winter and spring

316. *How should a billbergia be planted?*

In standard bromeliad soil (see 343) with about 2 inches of coarse drainage material in the bottom of the pot.

317. *Why doesn't my billbergia bloom?*

Something must be wrong because this plant rarely fails to produce flowers. Perhaps your problem is too little light or too much water. Billbergias require strong light and some sun. In spring and summer, when growing actively, they need a lot of water at the roots and frequent spraying of tops. In winter, give less water.

318. *Is billbergia a good plant for a hanging basket?*

Yes, it is an air plant and seems to do better in a hanging basket, where it gets good air circulation, than in a pot in a crowded window.

BIRD-OF-PARADISE (*Strelitzia reginae*)

Tall South African plant with striking, blue-streaked, orange-yellow, summer and fall flowers that do look like birds

319. *How can I grow bird-of-paradise plant successfully?*

This big plant needs a very large pot, perhaps a tub, since it requires lots of growing room. It will not bloom until it attains some size. Give full sun and a cool place in winter (55° to 65°F). Keep well watered through the spring and when buds start to appear in summer, but keep on the dry side during late fall and winter when the plant rests.

320. *Should bird-of-paradise be moved outdoors in the summer?*

Yes, if the temperature does not drop below about 55°F. Plunge the pot in the ground up to its rim and water and feed regularly. Or keep the plant on the porch or terrace.

321. *Why doesn't my good-sized bird-of-paradise plant bloom?*

Plants rarely bloom until they have at least seven leaves and a big root system somewhat pot-bound.

322. *How can I get bird-of-paradise seeds to germinate?*

They naturally take a long time—four to eight weeks, sometimes longer. Sow in a mixture of sand and peat moss and keep moist. If you nick the seeds with a file before sowing, it may speed them up.

BLOOD LEAF (*Iresine herbsti*)

Tall tropical shrub with showy purple-red leaves with red veins

323. *What are the needs of the blood-leaf plant?*

Normal house temperature, ample moisture but not a soggy soil, general-purpose soil (see 1). Set outdoors in summer.

324. *How can I get back the rich coloring of blood-leaf foliage?*

Give the plant the full sun of a south window.

BONSAI

Traditional Japanese bonsai are hardy trees and shrubs kept dwarf and trained to interesting shapes, but woody tropical plants can be trained the same way

325. *Why did my pine bonsai die after it was moved indoors this winter?*

True bonsai are not indoor plants. You can bring them indoors for a day or so during moderate weather; but like normal trees and shrubs, their proper year-round home is in the open sun and air.

326. *I realize that true bonsai are hardy plants that must be kept outdoors; but isn't it possible to train tender plants as bonsai?*

Indeed yes. Many tropical trees and shrubs can be trained in this way. The difference between them and Japanese bonsai is that they are grown indoors, and if they are put outdoors at all, it is only when the weather is mild.

327. *Would a tropical tree—say a silk oak—trained like bonsai and a silk oak growing naturally require different indoor growing conditions?*

The culture would be essentially the same, but the bonsai oak would be pruned more rigorously and regularly. Because of its small dwarfed root system and the shallow containers usual for bonsai, it would probably also require more watering.

328. *What is the best type of plant to make into a bonsai?*

Specimens that are naturally twisted or gnarled—the kinds that you would normally bypass—make interesting and beautiful bonsai. But by pruning and training, you can turn almost any normal plant into a charming bonsai specimen. Or you can develop bonsai by training a seedling, perhaps a maple or other little tree that has volunteered in your yard.

329. *How can I develop a tropical bonsai specimen?*

There is a definite technique and it takes practice. Read one of the books devoted to bonsai. In general, train the plant to the desired shape by careful and frequent pruning of the branches and proportional pruning of the roots (see 331-332). In addition, you may artificially change the shape of the plant by gradually bending or guiding it with braces and heavy wires.

330. *What is a good container for a bonsai?*

Any attractive container about 2 inches or more deep and preferably with drainage holes. But lack of drainage holes is not serious if you water carefully. And a deep container is just as good as a shallow one if it suits the size and shape of the plant.

331. *Can I train an old jacaranda that is vigorous but no longer attractive into an interesting bonsai?*

You should be able to dwarf it by hard pruning of the top and equally hard pruning of the roots (see 332). Do the job in several semiannual steps—a bit at a time—to reduce the shock. Train as you prune, and plant in successively smaller containers as you reduce the root system.

332. *How are the roots of a bonsai pruned?*

Unpot the plant, shake out the soil, untangle the small roots, and prune them with scissors. (*Illustration 16*) Cut away about as much top as roots; that is, if you reduce the foliage

16. Root pruning a bonsai

a quarter, cut roots back a quarter, too. Root-pruning is usually not required more than once a year.

BOUGAINVILLEA GLABRA (paper flower)

Woody South American vine with many clusters of lovely magenta, red, pink, white, and yellow flowers presumably in spring but frequently off and on the year round

333. *What are the requirements of a bougainvillea vine grown indoors?*

Use general-purpose potting soil (see 1). During the

winter, grow the vine in a sunny window; in summer, give some shade. Water enough to keep the soil evenly moist.

334. *Bougainvillea grows so luxuriantly in Florida—won't it get out of hand indoors?*

Not if you keep it well pruned. Flowers are borne on new growth only. Therefore, to maintain bloom and to prevent rampant growth, cut the flowering stems back to the main stems after the blooms die.

335. *Why haven't I been able to propagate bougainvillea from the young green stems?*

You should use the woody brown stems. Start them in water or in moist sand and peat moss.

BOUVARDIA

A rather large tropical American shrub with red or white, trumpet-shaped flowers that bring a delightful fragrance to a room or window garden in late fall and early winter

336. *Is the sun porch the best location for bouvardia?*

It should be, because bouvardia requires full sun. It grows in general-purpose soil (see 1) and needs plenty of moisture.

337. *What temperature does the bouvardia prefer?*

It must be grown cool at 60°F. Move it outdoors in late spring and bring it in again before frost.

338. *Should bouvardia be rested after flowering?*

Yes. After flowering in late fall and early winter, let the plant rest until early spring. Keep quite dry during this period.

339. *When should bouvardia be pruned?*

In the spring, when you move it outside. This shrub has a potential height of about 4 feet, and although it rarely attains this indoors, it does need annual pruning to keep it bushy and under control.

BOWIEA VOLUBILIS

Also called climbing onion and (mistakenly) *Schizobasopsis volubilis,* a bulbous succulent that annually develops into a long, branching vine

340. *How should bowiea be planted?*

Bowiea requires a porous soil, a dry atmosphere, and full sun. Use the same potting soil as for cacti (see 360). Bury only the lower third of the bulb. Keep the soil damp while the plant is growing in winter, but withhold water when growth stops in late summer.

341. *Should I repot a bowiea bulb when growth stops?*

Bowiea does well for many years without repotting. If eventually a larger pot is required, take up the bulb when growth dies down in summer, dry it off, and repot in October.

BROMELIADS

Members of the pineapple family. Forty genera of herbs—many of them epiphytes or air plants growing on trees but not taking nourishment from them—all grown for their foliage and some for their flowers. Genera listed in this book are *Acanthostachys strobilacea, Aechmea, Billbergia nutans, Cryptanthus,* flaming sword, *Guzmania, Neoregelia,* pineapple, *Tillandsia*

342. *Are bromeliads easy to grow indoors?*

They are among the easiest of all house plants, adaptable and obliging. Most of them are extremely attractive.

343. *How are bromeliads potted?*

In a mixture of equal parts osmunda fiber and sharp sand. Provide a good layer of coarse drainage material in the bottom of the pot. Plant so the soil just covers the stubby, hard growth *below* the base of the leaves. Press the potting mixture firmly down around the roots.

344. *How often should bromeliads be watered?*

Bromeliads hold water in a cup or vase formed by their leaves (and are therefore often called "living vases"). Keep this full and the soil always slightly damp but not soaked. Spray the plants with a fine mist about twice a week.

345. *Would the excessive alkalinity of our water have anything to do with the poor growth of my bromeliads?*

Yes. They do not thrive on very alkaline water or very acid water. Try to collect enough rain water, and when the weather is suitable, put the plant out in the rain occasionally.

346. *Is it true that bromeliads can be used as vases for cut flowers?*

Those that hold water in a fairly wide cup can be, but be careful not to bruise the plant when you use it in this way.

347. *How should bromeliads be fertilized?*

They require very little feeding—at most, only once a month during a growing period and then at only half the manufacturer's recommended strength for other plants. Many bromeliad fanciers recommend spraying the foliage with a foliar fertilizer or "leaf food" because in nature these plants take in nourishment almost entirely through their leaves. Commercial foliar preparations are available at garden supply stores.

348. *Will bromeliads grow in dark corners as is often claimed?*

No. They require sun in winter but a little shading in summer. They do best in an east window.

349. *What is a good temperature for bromeliads?*

Up to about 70°F, or a little higher, during the day; down to as low as 50°F at night.

350. *What will get rid of the hard black scale on some of my bromeliads?*

Spray with malathion. This will also get rid of other types of scale.

351. *How are bromeliads propagated?*

By offshoots produced around the base. You can cut or carefully break these off from the parent plant and pot them in the standard bromeliad soil mixture (see 343). The base of the offshoot should be rather woody and hard when the cutting is taken. Pack osmunda fiber tight around it to hold it upright until it roots well.

352. *Should I plant seed gathered from my bromeliads immediately or should it ripen?*

Dry it and plant as soon as possible. Bromeliad seeds are not viable for very long.

353. *How are bromeliads grown from seed?*

Sprinkle seed on moist sand and peat moss in a pot or flat. Press very lightly, but do not cover with the mixture. Keep in a dim place, covered with glass or polyethylene film until the seeds germinate (apply bottom heat if possible); then move into light but not sun. Transplant into individual pots as the seedlings become crowded.

BROWALLIA SPECIOSA MAJOR

Small, trailing South American annual with blue flowers—nice for the front of a window garden in fall and winter

354. *Why does a healthy browallia plant bloom so sparsely?*

Like other annuals indoors, browallia needs full sun, and this one must also be grown cool (about 60°F).

355. *When should browallia seeds be planted for indoor bloom?*

Any time during the summer (see 240). Bring the young plants indoors before frost.

BRUNFELSIA CALYCINA FLORIBUNDA
(yesterday-today-and-tomorrow plant)

Sometimes known as chameleon plant, tropical American evergreen shrub with tube-shaped blooms that start out violet and fade to white in winter and spring

356. *What is the best way to grow brunfelsia?*

Use a general-purpose soil (see 1) with a little extra humus and keep evenly moist. Grow in an east or south window with shade from summer sun at midday. Keep plant slightly pot-bound to improve the bloom. The day temperature should be up to 70°F. Don't permit temperature lower than 55°F at night.

357. *What about pruning and propagating brunfelsia?*

Prune this delightful winter bloomer in late spring or

summer. Take cuttings of new wood at this time and propagate them in moist sand.

BRYOPHYLLUM (air plant)

Succulents from Madagascar that produce plantlets at the leaf tips and with pink, red, or yellow flowers in winter

358. *Is bryophyllum difficult to grow?*

No, it is easy. Plant in general-purpose soil (see 1) and keep well watered. Give plenty of sun and a temperature between 60° and 70°F.

359. *How is bryophyllum propagated?*

Remove the little plantlets from the uncut leaves and plant in standard cactus soil (see 360). You can also cut off a leaf and pin it down on moist sand or even to a window curtain. Little plants will start in the notches.

CACTI, DESERT

Innumerable types of desert plants that require little water. Among the best for window gardens are *Astrophytum,* dumpling cactus (*Lophophora williamsi*), Easter lily cactus (*Echinopsis*), golden barrel cactus (*Echinocactus grusoni*), night-blooming cereus, *Notocactus,* peanut cactus (*Chamaecereus silvestri*), pincushion cactus (*Mammillaria*), *Rebutia,* striped chin cactus (*Gymnocalycium mihanovichi*)

360. *Exactly how sandy should the soil for desert cacti be?*

An excellent mixture for most cacti consists of 2 parts sandy loam, 1 part sand, and 1 part leaf mold. If your loam is not sandy, increase the amount of pure sand about 50 per cent. Cacti are not fussy about soil, but do need a somewhat richer mixture than many people think.

361. *How do I pot a small desert cactus?*

Use a pot only 1 inch wider than the plant. Put a good layer of gravel or shards and a little charcoal in the bottom. Firm soil around the plant roots and then sprinkle a thin layer of small gravel or coarse sand on the surface so that water will drain away quickly from the base of the plant.

362. *When should a desert cactus be repotted?*

When it becomes root-bound. Repot in the spring as the plant starts into growth.

363. *How are newly potted cacti watered?*

Apply just enough to dampen the soil, and keep it damp until growth starts. Keep in a warm, lightly shaded place.

364. *How much should established desert cacti be watered?*

In spring and summer, water thoroughly when the soil surface feels dry. (Occasionally let the soil dry out to about ½ inch below the surface to prevent souring.) In fall, when growth begins to slow down, gradually withhold water. In winter, when plants are resting, water just enough to keep them from becoming completely dry and dessicated. At this time of year, apply water only on bright days, when evaporation is rapid.

365. *Is it safe to spray desert cacti to remove dust?*

Yes. Do it on a sunny day when the water will evaporate quickly. Do not expose plants to the sun until they are dry, because they may be burned.

366. *Should I fertilize desert cacti?*

Only when they are growing vigorously in spring and

summer. Use dilute liquid plant food and make several applications at monthly intervals.

367. *Don't desert cacti require a great deal of sun?*

No plants demand more. Grow them in a south window. In spring, if the window is shaded by trees, supplement the natural light with fluorescent light (see 84-89).

368. *What temperature is best for desert cacti?*

They will do well at normal house temperatures. But if possible, keep them in a cool room (as low as 45°F) in winter, when they are resting.

369. *Should desert cacti be put outdoors in summer?*

Yes. Plunge the pots in sand or gravel in full sun (see 82) and leave them there until frost threatens.

370. *How are desert cacti propagated?*

Start the small, globular types from seed in very porous soil in a sunny window. Start jointed types, such as the prickly pear, from cuttings. Just cut off a joint at its base and let it dry for two or three days; then plant the callused end a fraction of an inch deep in sand and keep slightly damp. When roots form, pot in standard cactus soil mixture (see 360).

371. *How are desert cacti grafted?*

Cut the bottom end of the piece to be grafted (the cion) into a wedge shape. Insert this in a small cut in the stem of the plant upon which the graft is to be made (the stock). Bind the two pieces together with raffia or soft cotton twine. Grafting cacti is very simple because, unlike most plants, completely unrelated genera unite readily. (*Illustration 17*)

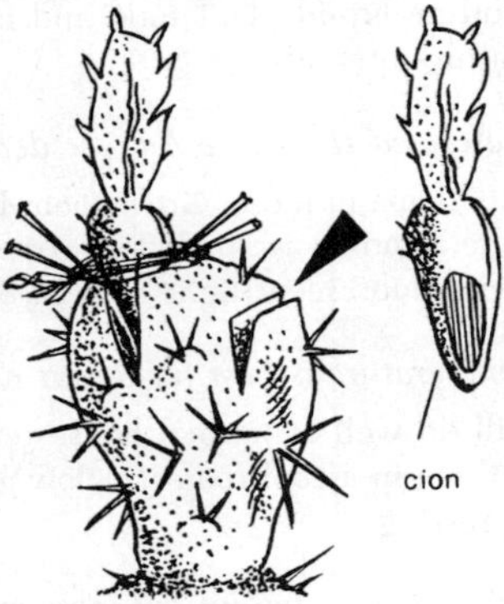

17. Grafting cactus

372. *Why has my cactus plant been at a complete standstill for a year?*

You have probably given it too much or too little water. Remove it from the pot and examine the roots. If these seem healthy, simply repot in fresh soil and improve your watering methods (see 364). But if the roots are dead or rotted, cut off the diseased parts, dry the remainder in the sun, and repot in fresh soil.

373. *Why should one of my cacti look sick even when I have given it the best of care?*

Root lice may be to blame. They are often quite a problem during a rest period because they thrive in dry soil. Remove your plant from the pot and examine the roots for white cottony masses. If you find any, shake off all the soil and wash the roots in cold water or dip in denatured alcohol for two minutes. Then repot in fresh soil.

374. *What sort of spray can I use on a cactus to get rid of scale insects?*

Any good oil-emulsion spray. Don't hesitate to use it more than once if the first application does not knock out the scale.

375. *How do I get rid of mealy bugs on cacti?*

Use a strong spray of water, then let the plant dry completely before returning it to a sunny window.

376. *Can I save a cactus that has developed a soft black rot near the base?*

Try cutting or scooping out the infected tissues and let the cut surfaces dry in the air until they have hardened. Then repot in fresh soil.

377. *Can desert cacti be grown in a terrarium?*

Yes. Cacti terrariums are attractive and easy to care for. To provide perfect drainage, spread at least 1 inch of coarse gravel under the soil and over this sprinkle several lumps of charcoal to keep the soil sweet. Place the terrarium in a light window. Water sparingly—about every two weeks. Cover with a piece of glass, but leave this open 1 or 2 inches to permit some air circulation. Remove it entirely if humidity within the terrarium becomes so high the glass fogs, and let the soil dry out before covering again. If mold should develop on plants, cut off infected parts and dust with sulfur.

378. *What species of the astrophytum cactus are recommended for the window garden?*

The bishop's cap is a 2-inch, spineless plant with pronounced ridges that give it a resemblance to a bishop's miter.

The star cactus grows 1 foot tall, has spines on the ribs and is covered with white tufts. Both plants bear yellow flowers in summer. Plant them shallow in a porous, sandy soil which is well limed.

379. *How should I plant the dumpling or peyote cactus?*

This small, bluish-green cactus with flat ribs, tufted hairs, and pink or white summer flowers has a long taproot, so plant in a deep pot—not the shallower containers used for many other cacti.

380. *Is the Easter lily cactus a satisfactory house plant?*

Yes, this small, spiny cactus with large, lilylike, white or pink flowers is raised like other desert cacti (see 360-377) but does not require quite as much sun. Give it plenty of water when it is growing in spring and blooming in summer, but keep quite dry if you winter it in a cold room.

381. *How can I propagate an Easter lily cactus?*

Remove the small offsets that girdle the barrel-shaped body and root them in sand (see 370).

382. *How is the golden barrel cactus raised?*

Grow this barrel-shaped cactus with many ribs, golden spines, and red and yellow flowers like other desert cacti (see 360-377), but keep it at 65° to 75°F. Expose young plants to only partial sun in summer.

383. *Isn't the golden barrel cactus too big for the home and doesn't it need frequent repotting?*

In about twenty years it will be too big—up to 2 feet tall and very thick through. Despite this slow growth, it needs repotting every spring before it blooms in summer.

384. *Can the night-blooming cereus really be considered a house plant?*

It grows well in the house and needs such protection in winter, but it is a big climber not overly decorative in winter when resting. It is, however, worth growing for its huge, fragrant, white flowers that bloom only at night during the summer. Several types of cacti are called night-blooming cereus, but the most commonly grown is *Hylocereus undatus.*

385. *How do I care for a night-blooming cereus?*

Keep in good light at all times. In winter, the soil should be almost dry, the temperature in the low 60's. In summer, increase the amount of water and give a little fertilizer. Grow in a mixture of 2 parts loam, 1 part leaf mold, and 1½ parts sand.

386. *How is the night-blooming cereus propagated?*

From seeds or stem cuttings. Let these dry in the air and form a callus before planting them in sand (see 964). Do not expect plants to bloom for two years or more. Old specimens bloom much better than young ones.

387. *Why doesn't my new notocactus bloom?*

Some of these small, round, ribbed desert cacti take four or five years to start flowering; others flower when much younger. In any case, once they start, you can count on an annual spring-summer display of red or yellow flowers. They are nice house plants grown according to the general cacti rules (see 360-377).

388. *Does it harm the peanut cactus if joints are accidentally broken off?*

The joints of this dwarf desert cactus with soft white

spines and red flowers in spring are very fragile, but no harm is done if you break them off. New ones take their place and soon crowd the pot. Propagate the broken pieces in sand (see 370).

389. *Does the pincushion cactus grow well indoors?*

Yes, this large group of cacti that are covered with tubercles tipped with spines and with small, bell-shaped, spring flowers of red, pink, white, yellow, and purple grow very well in small pots. Give them a soil mixture composed of equal parts leaf mold and sand with some gravel and lime added.

390. *Is it necessary to repot the pincushion cactus often?*

During their first four or five years, repot them in fresh soil every March or April, but use the same containers unless the plants have obviously grown too large for them.

391. *What are the cultural needs of rebutias?*

Raise these small, rounded cacti with lovely spring-summer flowers in many colors like other desert cacti (see 360-377), but do not let them become too dry in winter and shade them from the hottest sun in summer.

392. *Is it true that striped chin cactus needs a rich soil?*

Yes, this plant with valleys and ridges like a relief map, requires a somewhat richer soil than other cacti, but it must still be porous. Use general-purpose soil (see 1) rather than the standard cactus soil.

393. *How much sun and water should I give the striped chin cactus?*

Grow in only partial sun—an east or west window—and water somewhat more freely than other cacti, especially when the plant is making growth in spring and producing its chartreuse flowers in summer.

CACTI, JUNGLE

Small group of cacti native to the jungle, including the popular Christmas cactus (*Zygocactus truncatus*), Easter cactus (*Schlumbergera gaertneri*), orchid cactus (*Epiphyllum*), and *Rhipsalis*

394. Do jungle cacti grow in the same soil as desert cacti?

They require a richer mixture: equal parts loam, leaf mold, and sand. Put about 1 inch of coarse drainage material, such as shards or stones, in the bottom of the pot.

395. How much sun and water do jungle cacti require?

Less sun and more water than desert cacti. Grow in an east or west window or in a south window that is shaded at midday from the sun. During active growth, soak the soil thoroughly whenever the surface feels dry, and empty the saucers as soon as the pots stop draining. Keep on the dry side during rest periods.

396. Why is the bloom on my Christmas cactus so poor?

This hanging, spineless cactus (also known as crab cactus) is somewhat finicky. Do not move it around; set it in a warm east or west window and leave it there. Do not expose to cold drafts, and avoid hot radiators, too. Water carefully. In October, when the plant should be rested in a cool, dim place, keep it dry. Then in November water sparingly and when active growth starts within a few weeks, water two to three times a week. After flowering until October, water sparingly again.

397. *How much should Christmas cactus be fed?*

Give it a little dilute fertilizer every three weeks in the fall when it begins to grow actively and to set buds in anticipation of producing its showy red or pink flowers at Christmastime or soon after.

398. *What causes the leaves of my Christmas cactus to get yellow?*

It could be too much heat or water or too little humidity. It could also be too poor a soil. Repot in the standard jungle cactus mixture (see 394). Ordinarily, however, a strongly growing Christmas cactus should be repotted only about every two or three years.

399. *Should I move a Christmas cactus outdoors in summer?*

Yes. Plunge pot in sand or gravel in light shade and fill with soil so that water will run off. Rain will not hurt the plant, however.

400. *How do I propagate Christmas cactus?*

By tip cuttings taken before the plant starts into growth in late fall.

401. *How is the Easter cactus grown?*

This cactus is similar to the Christmas cactus but bears its red flowers in spring. It starts into active growth about January or February after a late fall and early winter rest period; otherwise it is grown in the same way.

402. *Is it true that orchid cactus does not like sun?*

No, it needs some but should not be exposed to hot midday sun. Keep it in an east or west window in winter and in the light shade of a tree in summer.

403. How much water should I give an orchid cactus?

These rather awkward, spineless cacti with large, variously colored flowers in spring need plenty of water and a little dilute fertilizer during the warm months when they are growing on the porch or in the shade of a tree outdoors. In winter, keep the soil quite dry, but spray the foliage with water on dry, bright days.

404. Why doesn't my orchid cactus bloom?

It may be that you did not rest the plant sufficiently during the winter. It needs two to three months of rest. Failure to bloom may also be attributable to lack of potash in the soil. Provide this just about the time new growth starts in spring (see 68).

405. How can I prevent bud drop on an orchid cactus?

Increase the humidity after buds form by spraying the plant in early morning and evening with a fine water mist. Avoid exposing to rapid temperature changes, and don't move outdoors until buds have developed full size in late spring.

406. How do I raise rhipsalis, the willow or mistletoe cactus?

These strange cacti with thin, ropelike stems or flat, leaflike branches, and insignificant white flowers are tree-perchers from the jungle. They are grown like orchid cactus but are potted in a mixture of 50 per cent jungle cactus soil (see 394) and 50 per cent osmunda fiber. Grow in hanging pots or orchid baskets (see 806).

CALADIUM

Tuberous-rooted tropical plant up to 30 inches tall with large, pointed, brilliantly colored leaves in spring or fall

407. *How can I get better foliage color in my pale caladium plants?*

Caladiums thrive in a soil mixture consisting of 2 parts loam, 2 parts humus (preferably leaf mold), 1 part sand, and ½ to 1 part dried manure worked in at the start. (If you don't use the last, apply liquid plant food at two to three week intervals during the growing period.) Such enriched soil plus good light with some sun and ample warmth and humidity will improve the color of the foliage.

408. *Why hasn't the caladium I planted developed larger leaves and bushier growth?*

It might be because the soil is not light enough (see 407), or there may be some other cultural lack: caladiums require abundant moisture, but not a waterlogged soil, a fairly humid atmosphere, temperature of about 70°F, and good light with several hours of sun.

409. *How are caladium tubers stored when the plants die down?*

As the plants begin to fade, reduce water until the soil is dry. Then store the tubers in their pots in a warm (not less than 60°F) place, or lift them and store in sand or vermiculite in a warm place. Keep dry. Start the tubers into growth again after several months—about March or later.

410. *Can caladium tubers be divided?*

Cut large tubers into pieces, each containing at least one eye. Dust powdered sulfur on the cut surfaces. Plant in a mixture of sand and peat moss; then, when divisions are rooted, move into 5-inch pots of standard caladium soil (see 407).

CALATHEA

Handsome tropical American foliage plants with brilliantly colored fluted leaves

411. *How can I duplicate the jungle conditions under which calathea thrives?*

You probably can't, but you can come close enough. Grow the plant in general-purpose soil (see 1) with a double quantity of humus. Give plenty of water, but provide good drainage so that the soil does not stay soaking wet. Provide high humidity and warmth of about 70°F with a little drop at night. Give good light but not much sun—an east window is a good exposure.

412. *How can I prevent red spider on calathea plants?*

Spray the foliage every week with water. Increase the humidity (spider mites flourish under hot, dry conditions). To get rid of mites, spray with malathion.

CALIFORNIA PITCHER PLANT (*Darlingtonia californica*)

Also known as cobra plant, an insectivorous plant that suggests a snake dancing to music

413. *How can the California pitcher plant be grown indoors?*

Plant in sphagnum moss or a mixture of sand and peat moss. Keep moist at all times (this is a bog plant). Grow in a cool east window, down to 45°F in winter.

414. *Is it a good idea to plant a California pitcher plant outdoors in the summer?*

Yes. If you have a boggy spot in the shade, plant it directly in the ground. If it must remain in the pot, be sure to give it lots of water every day.

415. *Why did the tall stalks of my cobra plant die back this fall?*

This is normal. They will soon be replaced by new growth.

CALLA LILY (*Zantedeschia*)

Tall, tuberous, tropical plant with upright, funnel-shaped flowers in white, yellow, or pink from Christmas on

416. *Why can't I get calla lilies to bloom?*

Plant calla lilies ½ inch deep in general-purpose soil (see 1) with an extra supply of humus. Use 6-inch pots for all except miniature varieties, which require 4's. Keep in a dim, 55° to 60°F place and water lightly until growth appears in about three weeks. Then move into a bright place about 5 degrees warmer, water twice a day, and feed at three-week intervals. Grow in a south window after the flower stalk develops, but don't allow heat much over 65°F. Growing your plants in this way, you should get satisfactory bloom.

417. *Can a calla lily tuber be saved from season to season?*

Yes, for years. One method is to keep the plant growing until July, then gradually withhold water, and finally, when growth dies down, stop watering entirely. Turn the pot on its side and store dry for about six weeks. The other method is to remove the growing plant from its pot in June and plant outside in the garden. In the fall, dig it up, dry off the tuber, and store for six to eight weeks. This long rest is needed if tubers are to produce bloom year after year.

CALLISIA

Ground-hugging creeper with variously shaped leaves white or yellow striped; in the species *C. fragrans,* leaves turn reddish-purple in strong light

418. How do you grow callisia?

Pot in general-purpose soil (see 1) and keep it evenly moist. Grow at an east or west window at 55° to 70°F. Pinch often to promote compact growth and cut out old stems entirely when the plant gets too large. Move outdoors in partial shade in summer. *C. fragrans* is easily propagated by stem-layering (see 142).

CALLISTEMON LANCEOLATUS (bottle-brush)

Australian shrub up to 6 feet with small, lance-shaped leaves and spikes of red flowers in May and June

419. Is callistemon easy to grow?

Yes, if you can keep it at 55° to 65°F. Grow in general-purpose soil (see 1) and full sun. Move outdoors in summer and prune lightly in August. Propagate from mature wood cuttings.

420. How often should I water callistemon?

Water when the soil feels dry; then soak it through and through.

CAMELLIA JAPONICA

Large southern shrub, originally from Asia, with gorgeous flowers in white, pink, and red about March

421. Can camellias be grown in the North where it is too cold for outdoor wintering?

If you have a sun porch or room where the temperature is about 45° to 50°F, they will do well. They cannot be grown in an ordinary living room and they do take up a lot of space.

422. *What care does a camellia require to bloom indoors?*

In summer, keep it outdoors in light shade. In September, bring it into a cool, sunny room. Water when soil feels dry and occasionally immerse pot to half its depth in order to give the deep roots plenty of moisture. Spray foliage with water daily if possible to provide the necessary humidity. Apply 15-30-15 fertilizer once a month from the time flower buds begin to develop until three months after flowering stops.

423. *Do camellias require an acid soil?*

Yes, in the pH 5.5 to 6.5 range. Use a general-purpose soil (see 1) with oak leaf mold for the humus.

424. *How should a camellia be pruned?*

To produce large flowers, remove all but one of the terminal buds on each shoot (leave the side buds). This will also help to prevent bud drop, which is brought on by high temperature and lack of water. Immediately after flowering in the spring, cut back branches just enough to keep the plant shapely.

CAMPANULA ISOPHYLLA (star of Bethlehem)

Also called Italian bellflower and falling stars, a trailing Italian plant with numerous small blue or white flowers from July to November

425. *How can I get campanula isophylla to bloom well?*

This will bloom from late summer into early winter if grown in a cool (65°F), sunny window. Keep the soil moist but not wet, supply some humidity, and feed about every three weeks. Plant in general-purpose soil (see 1).

426. *What should I do with a campanula isophylla after it is through blooming?*

Thin out the old stems to allow room for new ones to develop. Move to a cooler (about 50°F) room and reduce watering. After about two months, repot in fresh soil and divide the plant if you wish, fertilize, increase watering, and return to the sunny window in which it is to grow and flower.

CHINESE EVERGREEN (*Aglaonema simplex*)

Tropical Asiatic plant up to 3 feet with long leaves and insignificant greenish white flowers

427. *Is it better to grow Chinese evergreen in soil or water?*

It makes little difference whether this reliable, useful plant is in a vase of water or in damp general-purpose soil (see 1) with some charcoal added. Little fertilizer is required, but growth is somewhat improved by providing a fair amount of humidity. Keep potted plants in saucers of wet pebbles (see 92). Cuttings root readily in water.

428. *How much sun does Chinese evergreen need?*

One of the best things about Chinese evergreen is that it grows well in dim light. It will do better, however, if kept in a bright north window.

CHINESE HIBISCUS (*Hibiscus rosa-sinensis*)

Also called rose of China and China rose, a large tropical Asiatic shrub with hollyhocklike flowers in white, red, and pink in summer and fall

429. *Why doesn't my hibiscus bloom better in winter?*

This is its natural resting period. Bloom is best in summer and fall, but the plant is ornamental at all times. While it is resting, keep the soil on the dry side and do not let room temperatures go too high. When plant is growing well, water freely and provide all the sun you can.

430. *What shall I do with my Chinese hibiscus when summer comes? It has grown enormously.*

In spring, cut stems back close to the main trunk. Repotting in general-purpose soil (see 1) will probably be necessary. Give plenty of water when growth starts and spray foliage frequently. When the weather is warm, move pot outdoors to a sunny spot (see 82). You will probably have to prune the plant again in the fall before you bring it in.

CHIONODOXA (glory-of-the-snow)

Tiny spring bulbous plant from Asia Minor with clusters of blue, pink, or white flowers

431. *How are chionodoxa bulbs grown indoors?*

As soon as they are available in the fall, plant bulbs ½ inch apart in general-purpose soil (see 1) and put them in a cool, dark place. They are forced like other bulbs (see 148-152).

CHRYSANTHEMUM

Favorite, showy perennial from Asia and Europe with autumn flowers in all colors except blue

432. *Can I get bloom from chrysanthemums brought indoors in bud from the garden?*

Yes, for four to six weeks. During the summer, keep outdoor plants pinched back. In September, when buds begin to develop, water well and then dig the plants with a good ball of earth and set in pots. Spray with malathion to control aphids. Bring indoors to a cool (45° to 50°F), sunny window to flower. Spray foliage daily. After flowering, discard plants or cut back and plunge the pots in a cold frame so you can use them to supply cuttings in the spring.

433. *How can I make a florist's chrysanthemum bloom longer?*

You probably can't. Flowers will last about two weeks and buds will open for about two weeks more if there are a number of them and you can keep the plant in a cool, sunny place. Be sure to spray the tops every day with water. All chrysanthemums, whether florist or garden grown, need this attention.

434. *Can florists' chrysanthemums be planted outside after they have bloomed?*

The hardy types that bloom in early fall will usually survive if planted outside as soon as flowering stops. The big greenhouse types, however, will not come through in the North.

CIGAR FLOWER (*Cuphea platycentra*)

Mexican shrub up to 15 inches with short, tubular, red flowers with white tips in spring

435. *Is cigar flower a good one for the window garden?*

Yes, it does well in a 3-inch pot in general-purpose soil (see 1) in a cool, sunny window. Blooming plants can be had in a single season from seeds or cuttings.

CINERARIA (*Senecio cruentus*)

Low-growing plant from the Canary Islands with great

masses of flowers in all colors except yellow—a good florist's plant to buy for spring color indoors

436. *Why can't I make the flowers of a florist's cineraria last longer?*

Undoubtedly your house is too warm. No matter whether they come from a florist or you grow them yourself, cineraries bloom well only at low temperatures (60°F or less). Even then the flowers last only about two weeks.

437. *Can I raise cinerarias from seed to grow in a cool sun porch?*

This is not an easy plant to raise because it requires sunny but cool conditions at all times, but there is no harm in trying. For spring bloom, sow seeds outdoors in flats in August or early September. Pot seedlings in sterilized general-purpose soil (see 1) and bring indoors before frost. Keep plants pinched back and slightly pot-bound. Water regularly and apply fertilizer every month. For earlier winter bloom indoors, sow seeds outdoors in spring. Grow them in the coolest possible location, as on the north side of the house. Even here they may not react well to summer heat.

438. *Can I care for a cineraria so it will bloom next year?*

It is well-nigh impossible. Although a perennial, it is usually treated as an annual, so start new plants from seed every year (see 437).

CLERODENDRON THOMSONAE (glory bower)

Handsome, tropical, woody vine with red-and-white flowers in spring and early summer

439. *What sort of growing conditions does clerodendron demand?*

General-purpose soil (see 1) that is kept damp; a sunny window; about 65°F temperature; fairly high humidity (spray tops frequently); something to twine around as it climbs. In winter, keep the plant in a cool, light place and reduce watering.

440. Can clerodendron be trained as a bush instead of a vine?

Yes. The best pruning time, whether you are growing the plant as a bush or a vine, is early in the winter dormant period. Cut back stems pretty hard. Blooms come on new wood.

CLIVIA

Large South African plant bearing great clusters of scarlet, orange, or yellow lilylike flowers in March

441. Is the clivia difficult to grow indoors?

Not if you have plenty of room and a cool place. Pot in general-purpose soil (see 1). In summer, keep the plant outdoors in light shade; water regularly and fertilize every two weeks. Bring in well before frost and let the plant rest in a light, cool (55°F or less) place until about January 15. Meanwhile, water very little and do not feed. Then move into a sunny, warmer (65°F) location, water freely, and resume fortnightly fertilizing.

442. When should I repot clivia?

Not more than every three to five years. Do it right after flowering and give fresh soil to which it is wise to add some well-rotted manure. Keep in a warm (65°F), bright room and spray the foliage daily with water until you put it outdoors.

COLEUS

Also called painted nettles, bushy, tropical plant up to 3 feet tall with large leaves richly marked red, pink, yellow, or brown

443. *How can I grow a really bushy coleus plant?*

Pinch it back ruthlessly. Grow in full sun, which will increase the rich coloring, at normal house temperatures. Use general-purpose soil (see 1). Water and feed regularly.

444. *What can I do with a coleus that has grown very leggy?*

Coleus tends to legginess. When it has got out of hand, take stem cuttings in the spring and throw the rest of the plant away. The cuttings root rapidly in moist sand or in a tumbler of water and will make a fine display indoors by the next winter. Coleus is also easily grown from seed.

445. *What can I do about the mealy bugs on my coleus plants?*

Mealy bugs are a real nuisance with this plant. Keep an eye out for them at all times and when you find them, use a fairly hard water spray. Strong insecticides may damage the foliage.

COLUMNEA

Tropical American gesneriads with attractive foliage and tubular flowers in pink, red, or yellow in fall to late spring, depending on species; trailing types are lovely in hanging baskets

446. *I have been hearing a lot about columneas as companion plants for African violets. How are they grown?*

Plant in a sterilized mixture of equal parts loam, humus, and sand in clean containers with ½ to 1 inch of coarse drainage material in the bottom. Keep soil uniformly moist and spray the tops frequently. Grow in an east or west window at 70° to 75°F during the day, down to 60° to 65°F at night.

447. *Why aren't my columneas more lush and blooming better?*

The temperature may be too low (see 446) and you may not be providing enough humidity. Keep pots in saucers of wet pebbles (see 92) and mist the plants daily, if possible, with water.

448. *How can I get my columnea plant to fill out more?*

Cut out some of the woody stems. (Then, if you wish, propagate the tips in moist sand and peat moss under polyethylene film.) A better way is to promote bushy growth from the beginning by pinching back stems when they are young.

COSTUS (spiral flag)

Large Central American perennial, with long stems on which the attractive leaves are arranged spirally, and spring flowers in white, yellow, or red

449. *Is costus a good house plant?*

It is highly recommended if you can manage its size (some species grow to as much as 10 feet). Grow in well-drained general-purpose soil (see 1) in good light with some sun. Keep roots moist.

450. *What brings out the leaf color in costus?*

Grow in an east or west window and keep warm. This plant needs 65° to 75°F.

CRASSULA

Wide variety of mostly South African succulents, some large, some small, some with flowers at various times of year. A popular species is *C. portulacea* (jade plant—also called Japanese rubber plant and Japanese laurel)

451. *How are the crassulas raised?*

In general, like other succulents (see 957-965). Some that have a winter growing period, such as *C. lactea* and *C. multicava,* require more water at this season than those that are resting at that time.

452. *Why doesn't my jade plant bloom?*

Grown indoors, the jade plant is an erratic bloomer, and sometimes never blooms at all. It seems to be a matter of age, although young plants sometimes start blooming in spring if they are pot-bound. This is one to grow on the dry side.

453. *What might have caused a flowering crassula to die soon after blooming?*

Perhaps this was one of the annual crassulas, such as *C. columnaris* or *C. pyramidalis.* These must be started each year from seed.

454. *Is a Crassula falcata naturally a sprawling grower?*

Yes, this is fairly normal, but since the plant looks better erect, why not stake it?

455. *How can I get rid of a mold that is developing on a plant of Crassula lycopodioides?*

Fungous diseases like this can usually be prevented by proper watering and good air circulation. Watch out for over-watering and a close atmosphere. Remove affected parts with a sterilized knife and dust the wounds with sulfur.

CREEPING FIG (*Ficus pumila*)

Tropical Asiatic climbing vine with small heart-shaped leaves that lie flat against the support on which the plant grows

456. *How adaptable is creeping fig?*

It is very adaptable. It grows in general-purpose soil (see 1) in an east or west window in average house temperature. Keep the soil moist and spray the leaves occasionally.

457. *Does creeping fig need a special support to climb?*

No, it will cling to almost anything—even a slick painted surface. Spraying with water encourages it to cling.

CROCUS

Little bulbous plant from the Mediterranean whose bright, cup-shaped flowers in white, yellow, mauve, blue, and purple tell us spring is here

458. *Can crocuses be grown indoors?*

Yes, by forcing like other hardy bulbs (see 148-152). Plant in bulb pans about ½ inch apart, and for the best effect in the window garden, use one color to a pot.

CROTON (*Codiaeum*)

Tropical shrub with extremely handsome leaves of various colors and shapes

459. *Are crotons good house plants?*

They are difficult because they require high humidity and 70° to 80°F warmth. They need sun to bring out their brilliant colors, but if exposed to too much the leaves burn, so protect them from midday sun with a thin curtain.

460. *Why did the crotons I brought back from Florida drop their leaves?*

Probably because the humidity in your house is too low. Try to increase humidity (see 92). Use a general-purpose soil (see 1) and keep moist. Put the plants on a shaded terrace or porch when warm weather arrives.

CROWN OF THORNS (*Euphorbia splendens*)

Creeping, very spiny succulent from Madagascar with brilliant red bracts that bloom most of the year but most freely in winter

461. *Why does my crown of thorns drop its leaves?*

You are probably growing it too dry. This plant needs a reasonable amount of moisture (see 960) except during the last two months of the year, when it rests. At that time, watering can be reduced but not stopped.

462. *Shouldn't crown of thorns bloom all the time?*

If grown properly (see 957-965), in a very sunny window, it will bloom almost continuously, but it does slow down a bit in November and December.

463. *How can I prevent crown of thorns from making such messy growth?*

This is its natural tendency, but you can keep it under control by training it on a little trellis.

CRYPTANTHUS

Brazilian bromeliad with attractive, stiff, spiny edged leaves that are banded white, green, and brown. White flowers appear in summer but are not showy

464. *Is cryptanthus easy to care for indoors?*

Cryptanthus is most adaptable, stands considerable neglect. It does well in an east window at 55° to 65°F in winter, up to 75°F when growth starts in March. Plant in standard bromeliad soil (see 343) and keep well watered during spring and summer.

CTENANTHE

Erect South American foliage plant with large, attractive leaves variegated in some species, all green in others

465. *What are the soil, light, and water needs of ctenanthe?*

Plant in general-purpose soil (see 1) and keep evenly moist. Grow in good light but little sun—a bright north window is excellent.

466. *Does ctenanthe require unusual warmth to do well?*

Temperatures of 65° to 75°F are about right. Maintain a fairly high humidity by keeping pots in pebble-filled saucers (see 92).

CYANOTIS

Small, tropical African trailer with close-set, fleshy, fuzzy leaves and blue flowers in spring. Popular species are pussy ears (*C. somaliensis*) and teddy bear plant (*C. kewensis*)

467. *Is cyanotis an easy house plant?*

Yes. Use general-purpose soil (see 1). Grow in sun or shade (see 468) and at normal house temperatures. While plant is growing actively, water thoroughly whenever the soil feels dry; but keep slightly on the dry side in winter.

468. *Why don't I get flowers on my cyanotis?*

Probably because you are not exposing it to enough sun. Sunlight brings out flowers. If you can be content with the attractive foliage alone, you can grow the plant in a north window.

CYCLAMEN

Very showy tuberous plant from the Mediterranean with large single or double flowers in white, pink, or red in fall through spring—a florist's specialty

469. *Why didn't the cyclamen I was given open all its buds?*

Probably because the room was too warm and you didn't water it enough. Next time you have a florist's cyclamen, place it in a cool (see 470), north window and keep well watered (see 471). It should then bloom over a long period of time. Note, however, that if you raise your own cyclamens, an east window is better than a north one.

470. *My neighbor had a beautiful blooming cyclamen from Thanksgiving until Easter last year. Why did mine droop and die in less than a week after I received it?*

Compare the temperatures of the two houses. Chances are your neighbor's plant was kept in a cool place—an absolute necessity if a cyclamen is to live at all. It needs 45° to 50°F at night and really less than 10° higher during the day. In fact, it cannot be on display in an average room even for very short periods without flopping over. A room with the radiators off except in extremely cold weather suits it fine.

471. *How much should I water cyclamens, and what light do they need?*

During their growth period, they need a great deal of water but the soil should not become soggy. When plants put out buds, apply weak liquid fertilizer every three or four weeks. It's best to water and fertilize from below so as not to rot the crowns, but if you are careful not to flood the pot, you can water from above. Grow in an east window or in a very bright north window. To provide humidity the plants need, stand them on pebbles and fill the saucers with water just to the surface of the pebbles.

472. *How should cyclamens be planted?*

Plant the tuber half its depth in general-purpose soil (see 1) in July or August. It will probably make little progress until you bring it indoors in September, when it should start to grow vigorously.

473. *Can cyclamens be grown from seed?*

Sow seed in July or August in a pot or flat in a sterilized mixture of equal parts loam, leaf mold, and sand. Cover with glass, and shade. When seedlings have two leaves, transplant them into rows in flats in a mixture containing a double quantity of leaf mold. Give plants good light but no sun. When they begin to crowd, pot them individually in general-purpose soil. Repot as necessary to successively larger pots until 6-inch size is reached. It takes about eighteen months to get bloom.

474. *Can I save a cyclamen tuber from one year to the next?*

Yes, but your chances of getting a good plant the next year are only fifty-fifty. After the plant stops flowering in spring, withhold water gradually and let tops die down. Then put the tuber in its pot in a shaded place outdoors and water only about twice a month. In July or August, repot, increase water, and keep in a light (but not sunny), cool place. If you don't get vigorous growth within four to six weeks, throw the tuber away.

475. *What is causing the weak, twisted growth of my cyclamen?*

Cyclamen mites. Spray with malathion or treat the soil

with sodium selenate (see 110-111). If the attack is advanced, better discard the plant.

DAFFODIL (*Narcissus*)

Beloved hardy spring bulb that can be made to bloom indoors any time during the winter. Narcissi of the paper-white type are tender bulbs and are grown in a different way (see 751-756)

476. *What are the best daffodils for forcing?*

There are a number of named varieties that can be forced. King Alfred is one of the handsomest. Others recommended by the Dutch bulb growers are:

Yellow trumpet—Golden Harvest, Rembrandt
Bicolor trumpet—Music Hall, Spring Glory
White trumpet—Beersheba, Mrs. Ernest H. Krelage
Large cup—Carlton, Scarlet Elegance, Flower Record
Pink cup—Mrs. R. O. Backhouse
Small cup—Lady Kesteven, Edward Buxton, La Riante
Double—Twink
Triandrus—Thalia
Cyclamineus—February Gold
Jonquilla—Trevithian
Tazetta (Poetaz)—Cragford, Scarlet Gem, Laurens Koster
Poeticus—Actaea

477. *Why are the leaves and flower stalks of the daffodils I am forcing in a closet yellow?*

As long as the bulbs are in the dark, growth should be yellow. But when the plant is about 6 inches tall and you bring it to the light, stems and stalks will turn green. For more about forcing daffodils, see 148-152.

DICHORISANDRA

Tropical American foliage plants with handsome lined or colored leaves and blue flowers in spring and summer

478. *Is dichorisandra a good plant for a fairly dark room?*

You can't grow this or any other plant indoors in deep shade, if that is what you mean by "fairly dark," but it does not require sun. If it gets full light equal to that in a north window, it will thrive.

479. *What should I do with dichorisandra after it blooms?*

Let it die down or cut it back, as you wish. Water sparingly until spring, when growth starts. Then water plentifully. Do not repot more than once a year at most, because best growth is made when it is slightly pot-bound.

480. *How are dichorisandra plants reproduced?*

Divide the roots in winter or just before growth starts in the spring. Pot in equal parts loam, humus, and sand—the best mixture for this plant.

DIOSMA ERICOIDES (breath of heaven)

Bushy South African shrub about 2 feet tall with aromatic foliage and very small white flowers in late winter

481. *How do I grow diosma?*

Use general-purpose soil (see 1). Grow in full sun in normal house temperatures. Water when the soil feels dry, and then thoroughly. Prune after flowering to keep the plant compact.

DRACAENA

Often confused with *Cordyline,* which is similar; a tropical African plant with long, sword-shaped, yellow- or white-striped leaves that arch out from a central stem

482. *Does dracaena require sunshine?*

It will grow in a north window, but the leaf colors will be improved if you put it in an east window. Provide general-purpose soil (see 1) which is kept moist. Fertilize about once a month. Syringe foliage frequently.

483. *My dracaena sanderiana is getting leggy. How can I improve its appearance?*

This dracaena tends to legginess. Take cuttings for new plants and throw the old plant away.

484. *I have a dracaena that touches the ceiling and looks as if it could go higher, given the chance. What can I do with it?*

Air-layer the plant (see 141) and after the new plant has developed roots, you might as well discard the old one, or cut the stem into 2- or 3-inch lengths and propagate them, too, by laying the cuttings flat on moist sand or sand and peat moss. Young plants develop from the eyes in the stem.

485. *What is causing the yellowing of leaves on my dracaena?*

Probably red spider. Spray or sponge the foliage with water once a week, and preferably more often.

DUMB CANE (*Dieffenbachia*)

Also called mother-in-law plant, an 18- to 30-inch tropical

American plant with large, oval, upright leaves, mottled or striped

486. Is dumb cane really poisonous?

If the stem is chewed, the juices cause loss of speech for several days, but it is not otherwise poisonous.

487. Why isn't the dumb cane on my sun porch facing south doing well?

The porch may be too cold, too sunny, or too dry. Dumb cane needs at least 70°F and only two or three hours of sun (it even does well in a north window). Being a tropical plant, it also requires fairly high humidity, plenty of water, and regular feeding.

488. Can dumb cane be grown in water?

Yes, it will put out roots and live for quite a while. But it does better in general-purpose soil (see 1) that provides nourishment.

489. What can I do with a dieffenbachia that has grown too tall and scraggly?

Make an air-layer (see 141), or cut the plant to the soil line. It will come up again.

490. How is dumb cane propagated?

Cut the stem into 2- or 3-inch lengths, lay them flat in moist sand, and keep warm. A leggy plant can also be propagated by air-layering (see 141), but it may take quite a few months for sufficient roots to develop.

DWARF BANANA (*Musa cavendishi*)

Rhizomatous, treelike (to 6 feet) plant from southern China.

In greenhouses it bears clusters of small, yellow, edible fruit but it rarely does this in the home

491. What kind of soil does the dwarf banana require?

A general-purpose soil (see 1) is satisfactory, but the addition of extra humus improves growth. Plant in a wooden tub that can be moved outdoors into light shade in summer (see 37). Fertilize frequently, particularly in spring and summer.

492. What are the cultural requirements of the dwarf banana?

Grow in full sun during winter at not less than 65°F and keep the soil constantly moist but not soggy.

493. Is it better to leave the suckers on a dwarf banana or cut them off?

You can leave the suckers, but then the plant will make a large clump. To keep it more manageable, remove most of the suckers—and with some roots attached if you want to start new plants.

EASTER LILY (*Lilium longiflorum*)

Favorite spring-blooming (indoors) bulb with fragrant, pure white, trumpet-shaped flowers

494. Can an Easter lily I was given be grown outdoors?

Yes, if it is one of the hardy kinds (as it probably is). Keep it watered and in a sunny window after it has flowered indoors and then plant it in the garden in a sunny, well-drained location after the last frost. It should do well, and might even bloom again in the fall.

495. Which Easter lilies are recommended for forcing?

Lilies are not the easiest plants to grow indoors and most hardy types are difficult. The Croft variety of *Lilium longiflorum* is your best bet.

496. *How can I grow Easter lilies indoors?*

It is not as easy as in a greenhouse, but you may have fair success if you have a bright sunporch. In October plant bulbs separately 1 to 2 inches deep in general-purpose soil (see 1) in 5-inch pots. Store in a cool (45°F), dark place for six weeks or until growth appears. Then move gradually into full sunlight at 60°F and increase the heat slightly if you want to hasten growth, or lower it to retard growth. Keep soil moist while plants are growing. Feed every two to three weeks.

ECHEVERIA

Small tropical American succulents with thick, often grayish leaves generally in rosettes and orange or red flowers in spring and summer

497. *What soil does echeveria like?*

Use desert cactus soil (see 360) with some extra humus and sterilize it (see 17).

498. *How do I care for echeveria?*

Keep it in a south window at 55° to 65°F in winter and water just enough to prevent shriveling. Increase water when growth starts about March and fertilize lightly once a month until fall. Plunge pots outdoors in full sun (see 82) in sand or gravel when frost danger is past.

499. *Can the rosettes of echeveria be propagated?*

Cut off a rosette with a little stem and root in barely damp sand. Or take off single leaves and lay them on top of dry sand without water. Miraculously, roots will develop and you will soon have new little plants to pot separately.

ENGLISH IVY (*Hedera helix*)

Familiar evergreen climbing or trailing ivy from Europe with many variations in leaf form and markings

500. *Why don't I have better luck with English ivy? I thought it was easy to grow.*

It is easy if you give it the right conditions: Full light but little sun—a north window is excellent. A cool room (50° to 60°F), because plants simply dry up if grown too warm. Moist but not wet soil, a little fertilizer about once a month, and weekly spraying with water or a drenching under the faucet. And dip tops occasionally in soapy water to deter aphids, a common pest.

501. *What ails my ivy? It is stringy and has only a few yellowish leaves.*

Too warm a room and too much water will cause this condition, particularly if drainage is clogged. Better check these two possibilities (and see also 500).

502. *Will ivy grow well in water?*

It will, and is one of the best vines for hanging fiddle vases and other ornamental containers. Add a little charcoal to keep the water sweet, and occasionally dip the foliage in soapsuds to clean it and remove any lurking aphids.

503. *How is red spider controlled on ivy?*

This pest turns ivy leaves yellowish, sticky, and cobwebby. It can be controlled by frequent syringing with water and by dousing under a faucet or hard water spray once a week.

If the infestation is severe, spray with malathion; but you should not have to resort to this if you use the water treatment and grow the ivy in a cool place.

504. *When should I cut my outdoor ivy to get well-rooted sprays for winter indoors?*

Cut pieces after a mid-August rain when the plant is full of water, and cut many more than you need because not all will pull through. Take mostly 6- to 8-inch tip cuttings, but also some long sprays for your arrangements. Even if they don't root, many last through the winter. Wash cuttings in soapy water, remove any leaves that will be below the water line and so decay and foul the water, and put the cuttings in a pail of deep water outside in the shade or on the porch, where natural humidity is beneficial. These August cuttings root much faster than pieces taken later in the year.

505. *How can I take ivy cuttings to get stocky plants for an indoor planter?*

Take tip cuttings 6 to 8 inches long from vigorous stems, remove the leaves from the lower third of the stems and insert the stems in moist sand. Cover with polyethylene film and place in a bright but not sunny spot until rooted (see 133). Then transplant into small pots of general-purpose soil and fertilize lightly once a month. When top growth starts, pinch back the tips slightly to encourage bushiness.

EPISCIA

Large family of trailing tropical American gesneriads with brilliant foliage and flowers of red, orange, white, or lilac in spring and summer

506. *What is good culture for episcias?*

Grow in a sterilized mixture of equal parts loam, humus, and sand, which is kept evenly moist but not soaking. Give a little balanced plant food every three weeks. Put in an east or west window at a temperature of never less than 55°F. To provide the high humidity required, spray the plants at least once a day with water.

507. *Would it be all right to grow an episcia in a south window?*

In winter yes, but as the days get longer and the sun hotter, protect the plant at midday by a thin curtain.

508. *Why should one of my episcias seem to slack off flowering while it puts out runners in fine fashion?*

The production of runners (stolons) interferes with the production of flowers. Cut off the new runners and your plant should bloom better.

509. *Can episcias be planted in hanging containers?*

This is an excellent way to display them. Another good way is to train them to a light trellis or a conical support of chicken wire.

510. *Can I propagate an episcia from the runners?*

Very easily. Just pin them down to the soil in the pot or put a small extra pot of soil next to the pot in which the plant is growing and pin one or two long runners down there. They will soon take root, especially if you mist them with water once a day. You can also raise more episcias from stem cuttings and, if you are patient, from leaf cuttings.

ERANTHEMUM NERVOSUM (blue sage)

Also called blue crossandra, a rather large Indian shrub with winter-blooming spikes of sky blue

511. *Why has my eranthemum bloomed so poorly?*

Perhaps the plant did not get enough sun or enough water. It needs both. But it isn't fussy about temperature if it doesn't go much higher than 70°F and it does well in a general-purpose soil (see 1).

512. *Can eranthemum be pruned safely?*

Shrubs grown as house plants usually require considerable pruning or they outgrow their quarters. Prune this one back after it blooms to keep growth shapely and the plant not too large. You can propagate the shorter cuttings in moist sand.

EUONYMUS JAPONICUS

Japanese evergreen with glossy foliage variegated in some varieties. Although it grows large outdoors, it can be held to about 2 feet indoors

513. *How should I care for euonymus indoors?*

Pot in general-purpose soil (see 1) and water thoroughly when the soil surface is dry. Grow in an east or west window at 60°F or less. Prune annually to maintain manageable size and encourage bushy growth. Move outdoors in partial sun in summer.

FAME FLOWER (*Talinum patens variegatum*)

Small, erect southern perennial with succulent green and white leaves and clusters of rosy red flowers in late spring

514. *Is fame flower as easy to grow as I have been told?*

It is very accommodating, since it will grow in a rather hot and dry room and needs to be watered only when the soil feels dry. Although it flourishes best in a south window, it will do well in an east or west window. Grow in general-purpose soil (see 1).

FATSHEDERA

Large woody plant that is both a shrub and a climber, with big ivylike leaves edged with white

515. *I have recently seen the handsome fatshedera; what does it require?*

General-purpose soil (see 1) which is well drained and kept moist. Any light except hot sun. Fairly cool temperature —65°F at the maximum for best results.

516. *Does fatshedera need to be water-sprayed often like English ivy?*

No, it is not so afflicted by insect pests as ivy, but it responds well to weekly spraying.

517. *Can I save a fatshedera that has lost its leaves (probably because I had it in too dark a corner)?*

This summer put it outside in a shady spot and remember to keep it watered. It very likely will put out new growth.

518. *Will fatshedera climb by itself, like ivy, or must I guide it?*

You will have to guide it, because it does not have English ivy's clinging aerial roots. Train to stakes or a trellis.

FATSIA JAPONICA (*Aralia sieboldi*)

Large, bushy, evergreen shrub from Japan with big lobed leaves and clusters of small white flowers in December

519. *Is fatsia a foolproof plant, as I've been told?*

Just about. It grows with little attention. Plant in general-purpose soil (see 1) which is kept moderately moist. Fatsia tolerates normal house temperatures (and even considerable fluctuation), and will grow in any fully light location.

520. *I have my fatsia in a south window and the leaves are beginning to yellow a bit. Is this a poor exposure?*

Fatsia is not intolerant of sun, but if it is grown in a very sunny window for months on end, foliage may turn yellow. Since good north-window plants are relatively scarce, why don't you grow your fatsia there? It will do nicely.

FERNS

Popular but not always easy house plants. Favorites are birds-nest fern (*Asplenium nidus*), Boston fern (*Nephrolepsis exaltata bostoniensis*), holly fern (*Cyrtomium falcatum*), maidenhair fern (*Adiantum cuneatum*), rabbits-foot fern (*Davallia fejeensis*), staghorn fern (*Platycerium grande*), table fern (*Pteris*)

521. *What is a good soil for ferns?*

Fern roots are fine and grow best in a soil they can easily penetrate. Use equal parts loam, humus (preferably the woods mold in which they naturally flourish), and sand. Add a little charcoal for sweetness and bone meal for food. Make sure of drainage, for while ferns require a lot of moisture, they do not like wet feet, especially from stagnant water in jardinieres.

522. *How much light do ferns need indoors?*

A north window supplies plenty. Lightly screened east, west, or south windows are all right, too. Ferns need full light, but tolerate only a little sun.

523. *Do ferns need a warm room?*

They grow well at 55° to 70°F. If given much more warmth, insects may move in.

524. *Exactly how much water do ferns need?*

A great deal to compensate for the dry conditions that prevail in most homes. Do not let the soil dry out. Spray tops daily with a fine mist of lukewarm water and, to keep off insect pests, use a pretty hard spray once a week at the sink. Necessary humidity is maintained if you stand ferns in trays or saucers of pebbles that hold water just to the base of the pots. To ensure moisture for the lowest roots, stand large specimens once a week in a deep bowl or pail of water until enough moisture has been drawn up to make the surface soil feel damp. This and the hard syringing are very worthwhile.

525. *Do ferns need frequent repotting? Mine seem to fill the pots very quickly.*

If ferns are growing well, leave them alone unless examination shows they are getting pot-bound. Usually ferns are fast growers and need repotting once a year toward the end of the rest period in February or March. But large, older specimens usually do not need repotting more often than every three years.

526. *Isn't it best to put house ferns outside in summer?*

Yes. Plunge the pots in the garden in a shady spot protected from wind, rain, and dogs—or stand them on a protected porch. In either place they will need a lot of water.

527. *How can I propagate ferns?*

Most easily by division of the roots. Try not to mangle

the plant when you do this job—the fronds are fragile. Ferns that put out side shoots can be propagated from these, too.

528. *How do I eliminate the brown scales on the underside of fern fronds?*

If these are arranged in lines or clustered in dots, they are not scales but spore cases (*Illustration 18*). Leave them

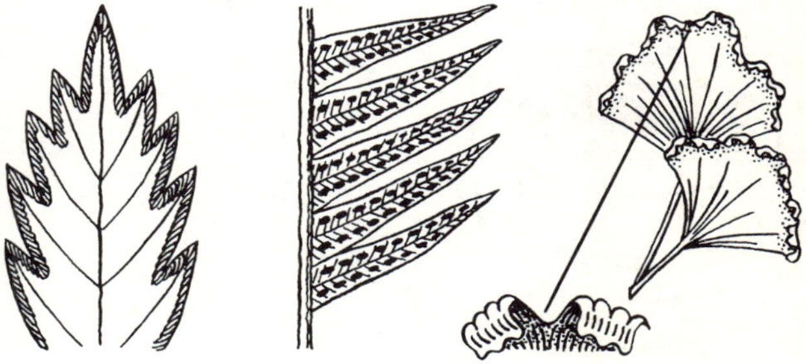

18. Arrangement of spores on fern fronds

alone; they represent a healthy condition. From them you can produce new ferns (see 529). If, however, the little bumps are scattered and on stems as well as fronds, they really are scales that should be eliminated by dipping in a soapy solution of nicotine sulfate.

529. *How are ferns grown from spores?*

Sterilize a pot or flat by soaking in boiling water. Use sterilized soil (see 17) and spread over it a thin layer of shards or bricks crushed enough to sift through a piece of window screen. Place the container in water until the soil surface is damp.

Just as the spore cases begin to open, gather the fronds in a paper bag and store in a cool place until the powdery spores fall off. Dust the spores over the soil, press in gently, and cover with glass or polyethylene film. Put the pot in a shady place at 70°F and keep the soil damp.

The first heart-shaped "plant" to appear is called a prothalium. From this the fern will come (*Illustration 19*). When

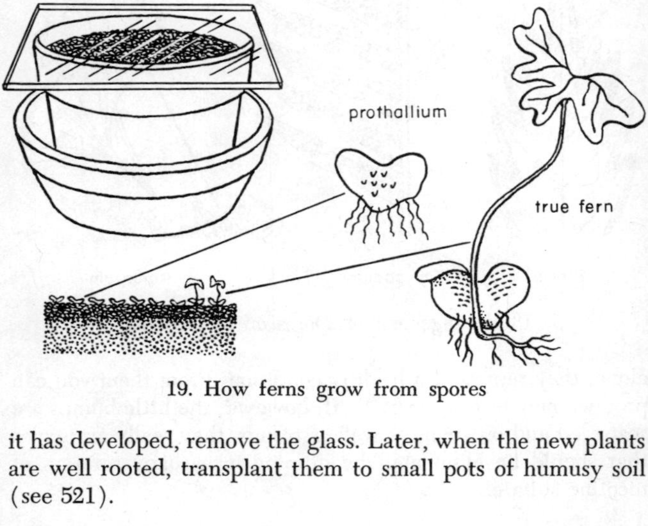

19. How ferns grow from spores

it has developed, remove the glass. Later, when the new plants are well rooted, transplant them to small pots of humusy soil (see 521).

530. How can I get rid of red spider on my ferns?

Try a strong water spray daily and then weekly for a time. This should break the webs and knock off the pests. Do not use chemical sprays or dusts because these damage ferns.

Do, however, try growing your ferns in a cooler place. Red spiders thrive in heat.

531. *Why do the leaves of ferns get yellow?*

Too much sun, too little fertilizer, too dry an atmosphere, too much or too little water can cause yellowing. Ferns require a good light but very little sun (see 522). In active growth, they need a little balanced fertilizer every three to four weeks. Some, such as the Boston, birds-nest, maidenhair, and table ferns, require rather high humidity.

532. *Why is my birds-nest fern so much smaller than those I've seen outdoors?*

Simply because you cannot duplicate in your home the ideal conditions under which this and other ferns grow outdoors. But if you give your birds-nest fern the care described in the previous questions (521-531), you will find it a very satisfactory house plant.

533. *What best suits the Boston fern in the way of soil, light, and temperature?*

Pot in a humusy soil such as the general-purpose mixture (see 1) with a double amount of humus. Grow in good light but with little sun at 55° to 65°F.

534. *I had no luck in dividing my Boston fern and raising the the divisions. What might I have done wrong?*

Boston fern is fairly difficult to propagate from divisions. Instead, pin runners down to the soil and cover with a pinch of soil (see 142). They will soon root.

535. *Is holly fern easy to grow indoors?*

This glossy, upright fern is one of the easiest, because

it is tolerant of more heat and less humidity than many other ferns. Follow general fern culture (521-531).

536. *Why is my maidenhair fern not growing well in good light in the living room?*

This lovely fern does best in a terrarium or greenhouse. It is difficult indoors unless the atmosphere is cool and moist —unlikely conditions in a living room. It needs a humusy, sandy soil, lots of moisture, full light, but very little sun.

537. *How can I make a rabbits-foot fern grow thicker?*

This graceful, lacy fern gets its name from the fuzzy rhizomes at the base. If you cut back or thin out the rhizomes as they creep out over the rim of the pot, the plant will put more energy into developing fronds.

538. *If the staghorn fern grows in trees, how can it be used as a house plant?*

Wrap the roots in osmunda or sphagnum moss and attach them to a piece of bark-covered wood. Keep well watered and it will accommodate itself.

539. *Why do staghorn ferns fail in my house?*

Quite possibly there is not enough moisture in the air. This fern needs a lot of humidity. Apply water daily at the roots and spray tops well at the sink at least once a week.

540. *Are any ferns adapted to a cool sun porch?*

The staghorn fern, with its antlerlike fronds, should do well if the temperature does not fall below 40°F. Of course, the plant should not be exposed to the sun.

541. *Are table ferns as easily managed in the home as their name implies?*

Yes, they are very good home growers since they are more tolerant of variations in temperature, humidity, and light than many other ferns. For best results, however, provide a fair amount of humidity, water well, avoid exposure to sun, and do not let room temperatures get too high.

FIDDLE-LEAF FIG (*Ficus lyrata*)

Also called fiddle-leaf rubber plant, a handsome tropical tree with glossy, fiddle-shaped leaves up to 18 inches long—excellent for a sun room or on the floor beside a large window

542. *Does fiddle-leaf fig need any special care?*

No, it is undemanding, grows in general-purpose soil (see 1) in normal house temperatures. But the broad leaves need occasional sponging to keep them clean and shining. Water only about twice a week in winter, when the plant is resting, but increase the supply slightly the rest of the year.

543. *Will a fiddle-leaf fig grow in a dim corner?*

It will last a long time, but like all plants it needs light, though not necessarily sun if it is to grow and thrive.

FIRECRACKER VINE (*Manettia bicolor*)

Fast growing, small-leaved, Brazilian vine with a year-round abundance of tubular, yellow-tipped red flowers

544. *Can I grow the pretty firecracker vine indoors?*

Yes, plant in general-purpose soil (see 1), keep moist, and fertilize about once a month. Grow in full sun except in summer, when it needs shading at midday. Give a reasonable amount of humidity in a room between 60° and 70°F.

545. *How do I train the firecracker vine?*

The vine climbs by twining around a support of strong cord, wire, or wood strips.

546. *Is it better to keep growing an old firecracker vine from year to year or start new plants?*

Young plants usually put on the best show. Root tip cuttings in the spring and keep them pinched until they have branched out. By fall they will be growing vigorously.

FLAME-OF-THE-WOODS (*Ixora coccinea*)

East Indian evergreen shrub with dense clusters of tubular red flowers from summer into winter

547. *How can I get better results with my flame-of-the-woods plant? It looks peaked.*

Perhaps you have let the temperature go too low; this plant requires a minimum of 65°F. Otherwise, it is not very particular, needing only some sun, moist general-purpose soil (see 1), fair humidity, regular feeding.

548. *Can a flame-of-the-woods plant be moved outside in summer?*

Yes, put it in light shade when the weather turns warm. It will bloom well. If kept indoors, screen from the midday sun.

549. *How can I get repeat bloom within a year from flame-of-the-woods?*

After flowering, water only enough to keep the plant from wilting. Then, after a month, cut branches back to one joint and resume normal watering and feeding.

550. *I'd like to give flame-of-the-woods plants to some friends. When should cuttings be made?*

Take cuttings in spring, each stem with four pairs of leaves. Remove the lowest two pairs and insert the stems in moist sand and peat moss mixture. Give bottom heat and an air temperature of 70°F. Keep shaded. When cuttings have rooted, move to 3-inch pots of general-purpose soil and shift on gradually to 6-inch containers. Tell your friends not to repot thereafter for two to three years, but to feed liberally.

FLAMING SWORD (*Vriesia splendens*)

Large, tree-perching, tropical American bromeliad with rich green leaves cross-banded in purple and bright red-yellow, and with spring-blooming bracts

551. *Under what conditions is flaming sword grown?*

Flaming sword requires a humid atmosphere and a temperature of 60° to 70°F. It does best in a greenhouse, but you can give the necessary humidity by growing it in a terrarium or keeping the pot set on a layer of wet pebbles. Grow in very good light but little sun. Water roots sparingly but keep water in the center of the plant.

552. *In what soil should I plant flaming sword?*

Grow in osmunda fiber or bromeliad mixture (see 343). The plant does well in pots or hanging baskets.

553. *Why don't suckers appear around my flaming sword plant as they do with my other bromeliads?*

This *vriesia* species does not send out suckers around the sides. A new plant appears in the center of the old one and gradually takes its place. Flaming sword is reproduced from seed.

FLAMINGO FLOWER (*Anthurium*)

Large, stately, tropical American plant with long, handsome leaves and almost constant flower spathes in creamy white, pink, red, or orange that stay fresh for months

554. *Does the flamingo flower require a special soil mixture?*

Plant it in osmunda fiber or in a mixture of loam, sand, leaf mold or humus, and sphagnum moss in equal parts. Provide a deep layer of coarse drainage material in the container. Fertilize with a little balanced plant food between the time one flower fades (after its incredible two- to three-month bloom period) and a new one opens.

555. *Why can't I get my flamingo flower to bloom?*

Your house is probably too dry. This plant requires high humidity and plenty of water, especially when buds are slowly forming and opening. In winter, grow in an east window at not less than 65°F, but move to filtered shade in spring and summer.

556. *Is it harmful for my anthurium to heave itself out of the soil?*

The roots tend to do this. Keep them covered with moist sphagnum moss to promote better growth. If the plant gets really out of hand, better divide it.

FLOWERING MAPLE (*Abutilon*)

Also called Chinese bellflower, a 3- to 4-foot shrub with maplelike leaves and very showy, white, pink, orange, red, or yellow flowers in spring

557. *Why don't I get more flowers on my abutilon?*

Perhaps your house is too warm or you're not giving full sun, an essential for this plant. Best flowering occurs when the plant is somewhat pot-bound. The roots grow fast, and when they are very thick, they need a great deal of water and a monthly dose of fertilizer.

558. *Why doesn't my flowering maple bloom as marvelously as the ones my grandmother grew to perfection?*

Probably your house is warmer than hers. A 50° to 60°F room is really best. Admit fresh air regularly to discourage mealy bugs, which can be a pest.

559. *How should I prune my flowering maple that has grown awfully big?*

On a big plant, the shoots that developed during the year should be cut back in September to about half their length. This will promote new growth and better winter bloom. You can propagate some of the cuttings in moist sand at this time.

560. *Can flowering maples be grown from seed?*

Easily. Sow seeds in late winter or spring. Keep warm and under glass until they germinate. When the seedlings are large enough to handle, shift them to individual pots with general purpose soil (see 1). Grow them outdoors during the summer. Before you bring them in in early autumn, pinch out all the shoots to promote bushiness and lots of bloom.

FREESIA

Tender South African bulbous plant with clusters of small, very fragrant flowers in white, yellow, pink, and violet from January to April, depending on time of forcing

561. *When should I plant freesias?*

From mid-August to November at two- to three-week intervals if you want a succession of bloom. Plant 1 inch deep in general-purpose soil (see 1), six bulbs to a 5-inch pot or bulb pan. Water well and place in a cool, sunny place, such as a cold frame or sun porch; then water lightly until growth appears; thereafter water thoroughly whenever soil feels dry. Freesias are a fair amount of trouble and not always successful as house plants.

562. *What is the secret of success with freesias?*

When cold weather arrives and you move the plants indoors, give plenty of sun and a low temperature (45° to 50°F). To keep plants from flopping, ring and crisscross the pot with wires or strings attached to a circle of 12-inch stakes.

563. *How do you save freesia bulbs?*

It is not advisable to do so because the bulbs are not improved by indoor growing. If you want to try saving them, keep the foliage growing as long as possible after flowers have faded. Then, when the foliage begins to die down, gradually withhold water. When leaves are gone, stop watering entirely and store the bulbs, in their pots, in a cool, dry place.

FUCHSIA (ladies-ear-drops)

Small tropical America and New Zealand shrub with lovely, pendulous, tubular flowers in rich pastel and darker shades usually in summer

564. *Aren't there any winter-blooming fuchsias?*

F. magellanica gracilis with red and purple flowers and honeysuckle with orange-red flowers bloom in winter. Or you can buy blooming or budded plants that the florist has forced. You may also get spring bloom from cuttings taken from large plants the previous spring.

565. *Why do I get such poor bloom on fuchsias?*

For about three months before flowering starts in the spring, fuchsias need cool nights (50° to 60°F); otherwise buds will not form. Perhaps your house has not been cool enough.

566. *Do fuchsias require a rich soil?*

No, they are grown in a well-drained general-purpose soil (see 1). But when they start growing after their early winter rest, they should be fertilized every two weeks with liquid fertilizer at half the strength normally used for plants.

567. *Is it true that fuchsias cannot be overwatered?*

Fuchsias need quantities of water when they are in active growth from about January to October, but this doesn't mean the soil should be soggy. Spray the leaves frequently with water.

568. *What year-round schedule should I follow with fuchsias?*

In summer, grow outdoors in partial sun. Before frost, move to a cool (45°F), not too-bright place and water sparingly. In January or early February, prune hard and repot in fresh soil (see 569-570), move to an east or west window at 50°F night temperature, water regularly, mist the tops, and fertilize. Move outdoors when danger of frost is past.

569. *Is frequent repotting of fuchsias advisable?*

Fuchsias need plenty of root room to grow and bloom properly. Repot into the next size larger pot when you prune (see 570). However, if you have cut the top of the plant back pretty hard, prune the roots in proportion (see 331-332); then repot in the old pot with as much fresh soil as you can fit in.

570. *Should I prune fuchsias every year?*

Yes, it will improve the appearance of the plants and strengthen growth. In January or February, after the plants have rested, remove dead and weak wood and cut back remaining growth somewhat. As the plants develop, pinch off new growth to stimulate branching but stop at least six weeks before you want or expect flowers. Blooms appear on new wood.

571. *How and when do I propagate fuchsias?*

Take tip cuttings in the spring or early fall and root in moist sand in a shaded place. Then repot individually and keep pinched to promote bushiness.

GARDENIA (*Gardenia jasminoides*)

Also known as cape jasmine, a Chinese shrub up to 5 feet with beautiful, fragrant white flowers from about January through June

572. *Why did the buds on the gardenia plant I bought from a florist turn black and drop?*

This results from the differences between your home and a greenhouse. The high temperature of the average home and the relatively low light and humidity level bring on bud drop.

573. *Why did the flowers on my gardenia turn brown? I didn't handle them.*

Lack of humidity is the most common cause. Gardenias need considerable moisture in the air to grow well. Frequent spraying of tops with water helps a great deal. Also keep the pots in pebble saucers (see 92).

574. *Is it possible to grow gardenias that will flower indoors?*

It is possible but far from easy. Even florists have their troubles, because the gardenia is a finicky plant. However, even without flowers—or with only a few flowers—this is a lovely foliage plant to have in the home.

575. *In what soil mixture should I grow gardenias?*

Use 1 part loam, 1 part peat moss (acid peat moss if you can get it), ½ part sand. A good substitute for peat moss is oak leaf mold. Be sure to sterilize the mixture (see 17).

576. *How does one maintain the soil acidity that gardenias require?*

Lack of acidity is indicated when the leaves begin to turn yellow between the veins. To correct this and to maintain the required pH of 4.5 to no more than 6, apply aluminum sulfate (see 13).

577. *I have heard that gardenias are fussy about temperatures. What range is recommended?*

The night temperature should be 62° to 65°F. The daytime temperature should be 70°F or just a degree or two higher. This narrow range of temperature is essential to the best bud formation.

578. *How much sunlight do gardenias require?*

Lots. Grow in a south window or a very bright east window.

579. *Should I water my gardenia heavily?*

Gardenias grow best when the soil is quite moist but not soggy. To keep the deep roots in good condition, set the pot in a pail of water every week and let it stay until the surface soil feels damp.

580. *Is it advisable to put my gardenia outdoors in summer?*

Yes. First repot it in fresh acid soil. Then plunge the pot in filtered sun in the border. Don't forget to keep it watered and fertilized, and spray the foliage daily with water in dry weather.

GENISTA (*Cytisus canariensis*)

Evergreen shrub from the Canary Islands sold at Easter by florists for its clusters of small, fragrant, yellow flowers

581. *How can I keep a florist's genista growing in the house?*

You can't; this is not a house plant. Just keep it in an east window at about 60°F until the last buds open. Then throw it out.

GERANIUM (*Pelargonium*)

Favorite plant of many types from many parts of the world with bright flower clusters and attractive foliage. Popular types are the zonals, colored-leaved, scented, ivy, Lady Washingtons

582. *Do geraniums want a porous or rather heavy soil?*

Neither. It would be better to say they prefer a firm soil. Mix 3 parts average friable loam with 1 part humus. Add sand if the loam is heavy. A spoonful of bone meal can also be added to each pot for enrichment.

583. *How should geraniums be potted?*

Provide a good layer of coarse drainage material in the

bottom of the container. Pack the soil rather firmly around the roots. Use small to medium-size pots for most plants—3- to 5-inch sizes.

584. *When should geraniums be repotted?*

Geraniums bloom better when somewhat root-bound, so don't shift to larger pots until the plants obviously require it by stopping growth.

585. *How often should geraniums be fertilized?*

Start when they are well rooted and apply a little fertilizer about once a month. When growth slows up, as during sunless weather in winter, omit fertilizer.

586. *Is it true that flowering will be improved if you do not feed geraniums?*

No. They require regular feeding with a 5-10-10 or 2-10-10 commercial fertilizer or any other with a low nitrogen content. Too much nitrogen promotes stem and leaf growth at the expense of flower development.

587. *Why are the leaves of my geraniums turning yellow and dry looking?*

They may be growing too hot or too wet or in a stale atmosphere. They may also need more fertilizer.

588. *What has made my geranium suddenly put on so much lanky growth? The leaves look peculiar, too—a little too big.*

You are probably overfeeding. Geraniums require less fertilizer than many other popular house plants such as begonias and African violets, but they do need some (see 586).

589. *Is it possible to give geraniums too much sun?*

No. Summer as well as winter they require all the sun they can get. So grow them in a south window.

590. *Can I grow geraniums successfully on a sun porch that is quite cool?*

They will enjoy the sun but, while they will bloom to some extent, they will be discouraged from doing their very best by the low temperature. Geraniums prefer a 60° to 70°F temperature. Night temperatures can drop into the 50's.

591. *Why don't geraniums do well in my kitchen-laundry where sunlight and temperature seem about right?*

Perhaps the room is too humid. Geraniums like a little humidity—such as you find in other rooms of the average house—but the steam that you often get in a kitchen or laundry or especially a combination kitchen-laundry is likely to be too much.

592. *How should I water geraniums?*

Water only when the soil dries out; then apply enough to get the root-ball damp through and through. But do not let the pot stand in the water that drains off. Water should be at room temperature or slightly warmer.

593. *How much fresh air can geraniums stand in winter?*

They do best when given quite a lot of fresh air. But don't let room temperature drop too low (see 590) or expose plants to cold drafts. And don't grow plants next to icy cold windows.

594. *Does it hurt to spray geraniums with water?*

Spray them only about once a month to clean the foliage

unless dust collects and more frequent cleaning is necessary. Spray on a dry day when the moisture will evaporate quickly, and don't put the plants in a sunny window until they are dry.

595. *Should I move geraniums outdoors in summer?*

Cut back large plants to a third of their size, knock off some of the soil about the roots and repot in the same size pot, if possible. Prune smaller plants lightly and repot if the roots fill the pot. Then set the plants in the sun if you want summer bloom; but if you want to hold them for strong winter bloom, keep in light shade.

596. *In the fall can I bring in geraniums that are blooming well in the garden?*

Yes, but if they have been planted directly in a flower bed or window box, they will require considerable root pruning to fit into pots, and the tops must be cut back to keep them in balance with the roots. This means you won't have bloom for some months—hardly before the end of February.

597. *Should I store geraniums in a dark basement when I bring them in from the garden?*

Absolutely not. Keep them in a sunny window and water just enough to prevent the soil from drying out completely. Do not fertilize. When they start growing again, about the first of the year, follow normal cultural procedures (see 582-594).

598. *Will potted geraniums that have bloomed well outdoors during the summer continue to bloom indoors?*

For a short time buds will continue to open. Then plants will take a rest. For year-round bloom, take cuttings in the spring and don't depend on old garden plants to flower on and on.

599. *At what time of year should I take geranium slips for bloom next winter?*

About June 1. You should then have bloom from about September on.

600. *What is the best medium in which to root geranium slips?*

You can root them in a tumbler of water, but moist sand or a moist mixture of half sand and half peat moss is quicker and produces a better root system. Put cuttings in a good light but not sun.

601. *What part of the geranium plant is best for making cuttings?*

The end growth. Take pieces that break part way through when you bend them.

602. *Do the general rules for growing geraniums apply to the zonal types?*

Yes, these familiar plants with huge, brilliant flower heads from about April to October are most adaptable. As long as they have sun, coolish temperature, snug pots and ample room to develop, and a reasonable amount of water, fresh air, and humidity you can hardly miss with them. See 582-601.

603. *How can I get brighter color in the foliage of colored-leaved geraniums?*

Grow these geraniums as you do other types. They need plenty of sun to produce the most brightly colored foliage (as well as their spring-summer flowers). If you overwater or overfeed, the colors are less brilliant.

604. *Should I pot up scented geraniums in standard geranium soil?*

They prefer a lighter soil. Use 3 parts loam with 1 part sand and 1 part humus.

605. *How can I prevent scented geraniums from growing so tall?*

Keep these fragrant plants with March-October flowers pot-bound. When they eventually need a change of quarters, knock some of the old soil from the root-ball and repot in fresh soil in the same container.

606. *Are ivy geraniums handled like other types?*

In early winter, the ivies require less fertilizer because they grow rather slowly; but as they approach their flowering period, beginning in February, give more food. In summer, place them outdoors in full sun and nourish well but be prepared for trouble if the weather is too hot and humid. Make cuttings in the fall.

607. *Why don't Lady Washington geraniums do well for me?*

In our colder climates, the spectacular Lady Washingtons with their gorgeous spring and summer bloom are primarily florist plants and they react poorly to the move into high home temperatures. But you can do pretty well with them if you grow them in a cool (55° to 65°F at the maximum), sunny window. Spray with water weekly to prevent white fly infestations.

608. *Should a Lady Washington geranium be moved outdoors in warm weather?*

Plunge the pot in a somewhat sunny border; feed a bit more heavily than usual in June and again in July. When you bring the plant indoors before frost, cut it back to about 5 inches and set in a cool (40° to 50°F) place in good light with some sun. Do not water much until February. Then move the plant to a sunny, 55° to 60°F window. Fertilize every two weeks.

609. *Overnight one branch of a zonal geranium turned yellow and wilted. About a day later, the stem looked watery. What is this disease and how can I cure it?*

This is bacterial stem rot and it cannot be cured. Destroy the plant immediately. Rot is extremely infectious, so after you have handled the plant, wash your hands thoroughly and disinfect any tools you have used with bichloride of mercury solution (very poisonous).

610. *What causes the leaves of a geranium to go limp and have grayish-brown spots?*

The condition is caused by botrytis. You probably can save the plant by spraying every week with captan until the plant is cured.

611. *What do I do about a geranium that has developed curled or crinkled leaves with pale spots?*

Destroy it. Leaf curl, as this disease is called, cannot be cured; but fortunately it does not seem to spread. But don't take cuttings from an infected plant because the new plants will be sick, too.

612. *Is there any one insecticide that can take care of all or most insect pests attacking geraniums?*

Malathion is a good all-purpose spray. You should not have to use it often, because insects trouble geraniums very little unless they are grown too warm or in a humid atmosphere.

GERMAN IVY (*Senecio mikanioides*)

Climbing plant from South Africa resembling English ivy but with thinner leaves and small, yellow, winter flowers

613. *How should I grow German ivy?*

Plant in general-purpose soil (see 1) and water regularly. Keep in an east or west window at 50° to 60°F. Propagate from end cuttings in water or moist sand in winter.

GESNERIADS

Large family of tropical plants which are becoming increasingly popular because of their lovely flowers and attractive foliage

614. *What gesneriads are recommended for indoor culture?*

African violets and gloxinias, of course. But there are many others including *Achimenes, Aeschynanthus, Columnea, Episcia, Gloxinera, Kohleria, Nautilocalyx, Rechsteineria, Sinningia, Smithiantha,* and *Streptocarpus.* Specific information for raising all of these is given in this section of the book. See index.

GLORIOSA

Also known as glory lily, a tuberous-rooted vine from tropical Africa with red or yellow, lilylike flowers in summer

615. *When should I plant gloriosa?*

In February or March. It should bloom in about ten weeks if the pot is placed over mild heat; will take two to four weeks longer otherwise. Plant the long tuber on a slant, eye up, and 2 to 3 inches deep in general-purpose soil (see 1). Place in a sunny window at 60° to 70°F. Water very little until growth appears, then water freely. Move outdoors into partial sun in summer if possible.

GLOXINERA

Tuberous gesneriad with masses of trumpet-shaped, rosy flowers in spring

616. *How is a gloxinera different from a gloxinia and is it grown in the same way?*

Gloxinera is a cross between species of *Sinningia* and *Rechsteineria*, but it is grown in the same way as gloxinia (see 618-647).

617. *After a gloxinera is through flowering, what should I do with it?*

Gradually withhold water, and when foliage dies down, store the tuber in its pot in a dry place for several months. Do not water. Then bring into growth again.

GLOXINIA (*Sinningia speciosa*)

Low-growing, wide-spreading, tuberous gesneriad from Brazil with furry, multiveined leaves and large, bell-shaped, winter, spring, and summer flowers in white, pink, red, and purple

618. *What soil should I use for gloxinias?*

Equal parts loam, humus, and sand with a spoonful of bone meal for each pot. Sterilize the loam and humus before mixing with the other ingredients (see 17).

619. *What size pots are recommended for gloxinias?*

Bulb pans are better than pots. Use 4- or 5-inch sizes for tubers under 2-inch diameter; 6- or 7-inch sizes for larger tubers. In all cases, put into the container ½ to 1 inch of coarse drainage material. Gloxinias, like other gesneriads, require perfect drainage.

620. *Can't gloxinias be started directly in pots? I have heard they were sprouted in flats.*

When a great many tubers are being started, there may be some advantage in sprouting them in flats of damp peat moss and then transferring to pots. But it is simpler for the home gardener to start the tubers in the pots in which they will grow.

621. *How deep are gloxinia tubers planted?*

The top of the tuber should just show above the soil.

622. *Should gloxinias be started in the light or dark?*

When they are ready to sprout, tubers will do so regardless of light or lack of it, but don't put them in the sun. Provide a starting temperature of 65° to 75°F.

623. *If gloxinias usually bloom in spring and summer, when should they be planted?*

February is the best month because the plants will develop faster than those started earlier, but you can plant gloxinias any time you like so long as the tubers have had a rest. With progressive plantings from August to April, you can have bloom from November to July.

624. *How long does it take for a gloxinia to come into bloom?*

About four months. Don't try to push it.

625. *How are gloxinias watered?*

When the tubers are first planted, keep the soil just moderately moist. As growth develops, increase the amount of water. When the plants are going full blast, water whenever the soil surface begins to feel dry—and then water enough to soak the soil through.

626. *Is wick-watering recommended for gloxinias?*

Many growers prefer it because it maintains the desired soil moisture (see 60). But remember that it's one thing to water plants this way and quite another thing to let "wickless" pots stand for hours and even days in saucers of water while they soak up too much moisture and the soil becomes water-logged and sour.

627. *Does water on the foliage hurt gloxinias?*

Not if you use room-temperature or lukewarm water and do not expose wet leaves to the sun. Regular spraying of gloxinia foliage is, in fact, recommended to clean off dust and provide necessary humidity.

628. *When should gloxinias be fertilized?*

If you do not use any fertilizer in the potting soil, start feeding as soon as growth starts, and continue at three- to four-week intervals through the flowering. If you start with fertilized soil do not begin feeding until about six weeks after growth appears. Use a balanced commercial fertilizer in any case.

629. *One of my gloxinia tubers put up several shoots. Should I leave these alone or nip off the extras?*

If you nip off all but one, you will have a stronger plant, better bloom.

630. *Will gloxinias grow in a north window as African violets do?*

Like African violets, they will grow but the bloom, if any, will be sparse and the plant will be tall and thin. To bloom, gloxinias need good light—an east or west window or a south window screened by a thin curtain from midday sun.

631. *Is it true that gloxinia flowers last longer if not exposed to too much light?*

If given good light but no sun, the open flowers do last a little longer.

632. *Do you recommend growing gloxinias under electric light?*

They do exceptionally well under fluorescent light. Before they bloom, set them 8 inches below the tubes. Once they start budding well, move them out from under the lights so you can enjoy them in the house in a fully light place.

633. *What heat and humidity do gloxinias require?*

A temperature of 65° to 75°F during the day; at night, down to 60°F but avoid exposing to cold drafts. As for humidity, gloxinias require less than African violets but certainly do better in a moist atmosphere than a dry one. Set the pots on wet pebbles.

634. *What should I do with gloxinias after they have flowered?*

Gradually withhold water until the plants die down. Then store the tubers in their pots in a cool, dark place for two to three months. If you do not have space for the pots, lift the tubers and store them in dry sand or vermiculite.

635. *When should gloxinia tubers be brought out of storage and started into growth?*

The dormant period lasts two to three months. But bring out the plants at the first sign of growth. Carefully remove the upper inch of soil in the pot in which the plant was stored and replace this with fresh soil. Set in a warm, bright place.

636. *How is it possible to get two blooms a year from gloxinias?*

Cut the plants back to just above the first set of leaves after they have flowered. Keep them in active growth and well fertilized in a bright, sunny window and you may possibly get a second flowering. Success is more likely, however, when plants are grown under fluorescent light.

637. *Why do my gloxinia tubers get smaller every year instead of larger?*

You are not growing the plants well. Give them sun, rich soil, proper watering—all the things just discussed—and the tubers will increase, not decrease, in size.

638. *Should gloxinias be repotted regularly?*

No, not until either the plant or the tuber becomes obviously too large for the pot. This will happen in two or three years if you grow the plants well and store them properly during their rest periods. Gloxinia tubers last for quite a few years and can become very large.

639. *Can gloxinias summer outdoors?*

When the weather is warm, you can move out plants that have not bloomed and they will flower beautifully. But it is not worth-while handling those that have already bloomed this way. After flowering, they are ready for a rest.

640. *How are gloxinias grown from leaf cuttings?*

Select small or medium-sized inside leaves. Cut them off so that a sliver of the main stem remains at the end of the leaf stem. Then proceed in one of these ways: (1) Stick the leaf stem through a hole in wax paper and set over a tumbler with the lower part of the stem in water. As soon as tiny roots form, pot in moist soil. (*Illustration* 8) (2) Insert the leaf stem in moist sand or sand and peat moss and cover loosely with polyethylene film (see 133). (3) Split the leaf stem lengthwise and plant in water or sand. It will form two tubers.

641. *I rooted a gloxinia leaf in water and then planted it in soil. Why did the leaf die?*

This is usual when a leaf is propagated in water. It often dies before a new plant appears, but if you had dug into the soil, you would have found a small tuber all set to grow in a couple of months.

642. *Can gloxinia tubers be cut in two and new plants grown from the divisions?*

Yes. Cut the tubers with a sharp knife and let each piece have a growing eye or sprout (to be sure, don't cut the tubers until after sprouts have appeared). Dust cut surfaces with sulfur or fermate and then plant the sections in soil.

643. *How can I grow gloxinias from seed?*

Use a shallow container with bottom drainage holes and line the bottom with a layer of crushed flower pots or charcoal, then a layer of finely screened soil, peat moss and sand. Set in warm water until the surface is damp. Then scatter seeds and cover lightly with fine sphagnum. Top container with a sheet of glass or polyethylene film and set in a warm, light (not sunny) place. Transplant the seedlings to individual pots of sterilized gloxinia soil (see 618) when they have four leaves. Do not expose the little plants to much sun until they are established.

644. *Why did some of the buds on my gloxinias suddenly turn brown, limp and lifeless?*

This is bud blast. It may be caused by too much water, too much fertilizer, not enough humidity, watering with cold water, or thrips. An expert can sometimes pinpoint the cause by examining the blasted buds, but in most instances, bud blast of house plants results from poor culture in general and poor humidity in particular.

645. *How can I tell whether gloxinias have thrips?*

The tips of the leaves wither; leaves are spotted silver-brown underneath; stems look rusty. If you do not take steps to control the thrips immediately, bud blast is sure to follow. Spray or dust the plants thoroughly with DDT.

646. *What is making the leaves of my gloxinia curl and the plants look stunted?*

Cyclamen mites. For their control, see 114.

647. *One of my gloxinia tubers didn't sprout and when I finally examined it, I found it partly rotten. It was a prize plant. Can the tuber be saved?*

If it has not rotted pretty much all over or if the crown is unaffected, you may be able to save the tuber by carefully cutting away the bad parts, dusting with sulfur or fermate, and letting the tuber dry in the air for about a week.

GOLD DUST PLANT (*Aucuba japonica variegata*)

Eastern Asiatic evergreen shrub with yellow-splattered leaves, purple flowers in March, and long-lasting red fruit in fall

648. *Where should I grow the gold dust plant?*

In a cool east or west window. Grow in general-purpose soil (see 1) and keep it moist. Repot in fresh soil every year; the plant should eventually require a tub. Small young plants are nice for dish gardens.

649. *How can I make my gold dust plant do better in the house?*

Gold dust plant needs a low temperature—from about 45° to 60°F, as on a cool sun porch.

650. *Why don't I get fruit on my gold dust plants?*

It could be that you are not growing them properly, but it is more likely that you have only male or female plants. Red berries develop only on female plants, and you also need a male plant to pollinate them.

GRAPEFRUIT (*Citrus paradisi*)

Familiar southern fruit tree grown indoors for its glossy foliage

651. *How is grapefruit grown from seeds? My child wants to try them.*

Plant ¼ inch deep in moist sphagnum moss, vermiculite, or general-purpose soil (see 1). Keep watered and in a warm, dim place. When little plants have a pair of leaves, repot in general-purpose soil and move into sun after a few days. Water when the soil feels dry and fertilize about once a month.

652. *Can I expect a grapefruit planted from seed to bloom and bear fruit?*

It may, but it probably won't. Citrus started from seeds are unpredictable and not very accommodating about blooming indoors.

GRAPE HYACINTH (*Muscari*)

Spring bulbs from the Mediterranean with small, dense blue flowers in grapelike clusters

653. *How should grape hyacinths be planted for forcing?*

Plant the bulbs ½ inch apart with the tips just at the soil surface. Follow regular bulb-forcing procedure (see 148-152). By planting in October you can have first bloom in early February.

GRAPE IVY (*Cissus rhombifolia*)

Climbing or trailing tropical vine with glossy leaves made up of three pointed leaflets and reddish tendrils—fast growing and decorative

654. *Is grape ivy a demanding plant?*

It requires constant moisture, but otherwise is easily grown. Plant in general-purpose soil (see 1) with some extra humus and place in an east or west window or in a fully light north window. It grows fast and does not need unusual humidity.

655. *What are the little waxy insects nesting between the stems and leaves of my grape ivy?*

Mealy bugs. They have a liking for grape ivy. Give the foliage a hard water spray every week at the sink to keep them under control, and pick off any you see, along with their egg masses, with a cotton swab dipped in alcohol.

GROUND IVY (*Nepeta hederacea*)

Fast-growing, creeping weed common to the northern hemisphere with small scalloped leaves all green or green and white

656. *Does a weed like ground ivy make a decent house plant?*

It is excellent for covering bare soil in indoor window boxes or planters and a nice little trailer for a pot. As long as you don't expose it to much sun or too dry air, it is easy to grow, requiring only average soil and care.

GUZMANIA

Tropical American bromeliad with basal rosettes of stiff leaves and white or yellow flowers in spring

657. *Does guzmania have any cultural peculiarities?*

It is grown like flaming sword (see 551-552). Give as much humidity as possible.

HAEMANTHUS (blood lily)

Tall, bulbous African plant with a large, round cluster of red, pink, or white flowers, like those of an onion flower, in spring and summer, depending on the species

658. *How is a haemanthus bulb planted?*

Plant in general-purpose soil (see 1) in a pot 2 inches larger in diameter than the bulb and with the upper third to half of the bulb exposed. Water very little until growth starts. Then increase the amount, fertilize every three weeks, and place in a sunny window.

659. *How should I handle a haemanthus bulb after it has flowered?*

Gradually withhold water after flowering and when the foliage starts to turn, stop watering entirely. When the foliage dies down completely, the bulb can either be stored in its pot in a cool, dark place or it can be lifted, dried off, and stored in sand or vermiculite for about three months.

HAWORTHIA

Small South African succulents usually with neat rosettes of thick leaves which in some varieties have translucent "windows." Sparse tiny white flowers are inconspicuous

660. *How are haworthias grown?*

With a bit more shade and less water in summer than other succulents, otherwise in the same way (see 957-965). Repot every fall in fresh soil because roots often dry and rot during the summer.

HELIOTROPE (*Heliotropium arborescens*)

Peruvian perennial up to 4 feet with small, delightfully scented purple flowers normally in summer but possible in winter

661. *Under what conditions does heliotrope do best indoors?*

For winter bloom, start cuttings in June or July in a soil mixture of equal parts loam, humus, and sand and shift to larger pots as they are required. Inside, grow in a very sunny but cool (down to 50°F if possible) place. Do not let the soil dry out. Spray the foliage on bright days and stand them in pebble-filled saucers (see 92) because heliotrope needs much humidity.

662. *Why has my heliotrope started to lose its leaves?*

The soil may be too dry or the plant pot-bound. Heliotrope needs plenty of root room and must be repotted often.

663. *My heliotrope was beautiful the first winter, but after a summer outdoors, it went to pieces. Why?*

This happens with heliotrope. Though a perennial, it does not bloom well after the first year. The best practice is to take cuttings from old plants in June or July. Keep flowers pinched off the new plants until you move them indoors in September. They will then bloom about March.

664. *How can I control the white flies on my heliotropes?*

These are a special nuisance with heliotropes but can be kept under control by spraying with DDT or malathion (see 115).

HOFFMANNIA

Tropical American foliage plants of varying heights with richly colored leaves

665. *Why should the leaves of my hoffmannia seem rather pallid in comparison with those of other specimens I have seen?*

Leaves are pale if plants are not well grown. Pot in general-purpose soil (see 1) with an extra amount of humus. Give plenty of humidity and warmth (not less than 65°F). Keep soil evenly moist. The plant grows in a north window but will have better color in an east window with some sun.

HOUSELEEK (*Sempervivum*)

Also called hen-and-chickens, prolific European succulents with thick leaves in basal rosettes and rather insignificant clusters of red, yellow, or purple flowers in summer

666. *Will ordinary succulent culture do for the houseleek?*

Yes, these are easy-to-grow plants, requiring fairly little moisture especially in winter (see 957-965).

HYACINTH (*Hyacinthus*)

Mediterranean bulbs with fragrant, showy flowers in almost all colors from early winter through spring. The Dutch hyacinths are the familiar, large-clustered type commonly grown outdoors. Roman hyacinths have more flower stalks with fewer bells

667. *Can all hyacinths be forced?*

Some are better for this purpose than others. These are good Dutch varieties: Edelweiss, L'Innocence, and Arentine Arendsen—white; Prince Henry—yellow; Orange Boven—salmon; Bismarck—Delft blue; Myosotis, Ostara, and Perle Brillante—blues of various shades; Anne Marie, Lady Derby, Pink Pearl, Princess Margaret—pink; Distinction, Jan Bos, La Victoire, Tuburgen Scarlet—red.

668. *How are the big Dutch hyacinths forced?*

The same way as daffodils. Plant from November to January. They will take about twelve weeks to bloom. See general forcing directions, 148-152.

669. *What are the best sizes of Dutch hyacinth bulbs to force?*

Use only the largest bulbs. These are graded as exhibition size, top size, or second size.

670. *The flowers of the hyacinths I forced are crowded in among the leaves. Shouldn't they stand out above the leaves?*

They should indeed. Where you went wrong was in bringing the plants out of the dark too soon. Do not expose them to light until leaves are about 6 inches tall and the flower stem is well out of the bulb (see 152).

671. How are hyacinths grown in water?

Use hyacinth glasses if you can get them; otherwise, any jar that will support the bulb above the water. Set the bulb over water that just touches its base. Keep in a cool (about 50°F), dark place for ten to twelve weeks. By that time, the roots should be well developed and the flower bud 2 to 3 inches high. Then bring the plant to a light room, but cover with a white paper cone for a week or more while the bud, leaves, and roots develop further. Then move to a sunny window.

672. Is it possible to grow Dutch hyacinths in bowls filled with pebbles and water?

Yes. The water should just touch the base of the bulbs. Handle as you would bulbs grown in hyacinth glasses (see 671). The important thing is to select deep enough bowls (at least 6 inches). Hyacinths—especially the large quality bulbs —make heavy roots.

673. Can the French Roman hyacinths be grown indoors?

Yes, they are forced in the same way as the Dutch hyacinths. Pot them in September or October and let them stay in cold storage for about eight weeks. They will bloom in three to four weeks after you bring them indoors—in November or December. If you prefer to grow them in water, follow the procedure outlined in 671-672.

HYDRANGEA

Up to 3-foot shrub found in many parts of the world with great clusters of white, pink, lavender, or blue flowers—a florist's plant seen particularly at Easter and Mother's Day

674. How can I get longer bloom from gift hydrangeas?

Keep in a cool north or east window and water every day or twice a day if necessary. Do not let plants get to the wilting point. Occasionally water them from the bottom in order to satisfy the deep roots.

675. *Can the hydrangea given me be planted outdoors and live?*

After it stops flowering, cut it back by about half and plant in the garden when the weather gets warm. If it is a hardy type (the way to find out is to ask the florist who grew it), it should do well. If it is not completely hardy, it will not come through in cold climates unless it is covered with soil during the winter—and even then you can't be sure of success.

676. *How is a hydrangea carried over from year to year for indoor bloom?*

Cut it back about half after blooming and repot in fresh soil in a larger container. Plunge the pot outdoors in partial sun when the weather gets warm. Fertilize and keep well watered. In the fall, before frost, bring inside and store in a cool (40°F) cellar. Water very sparingly. In January, bring the plant into a warmer (about 50°F), brighter room. Increase water somewhat for several weeks. Then move the plant into a sunny, cool (60°F) window and water plentifully. It will bloom at about Easter.

677. *Why isn't my hydrangea as vigorous as it should be?*

Are you watering it enough? While it is making strong growth in the winter, it may need water twice a day.

678. *When can cuttings be made from hydrangeas and how are they handled?*

Take cuttings in February or March. When they are

rooted, shift to 4-inch pots and plunge in the garden when the weather is warm. From there on, handle as in 676, and be sure to pinch back the growing shoots several times before July 15. You may have to repot once or even twice during the summer, and will definitely have to shift to an 8-inch pot in September. Use general-purpose soil (see 1).

679. *How do I keep my blue hydrangea from fading?*

Starting in January, give each plant a weekly cupful of aluminum sulfate dissolved in water at the rate of ¼ pound to 5 quarts. To make sure the plant absorbs this, stick a pencil or heavy wire deep into the soil at several places before you apply the solution.

680. *How can I turn a hydrangea pink?*

Early in August, while the plant is still growing, mix hydrated lime into the soil. A level tablespoonful will be enough for a plant in a 5-inch pot.

ICE PLANT (*Mesembryanthemum crystallinum*)

A prostrate succulent from South Africa with flat leaves covered with glistening dots and white or pink daisy flowers in summer

681. *How and where should I grow the ice plant?*

This old favorite is handled like other succulents (see 957-965). It easily adapts to the normal home atmosphere if given plenty of sun but not too much water in winter. Grow in a hanging basket for an excellent effect.

INDOOR OAK (*Nicodemia diversifolia*)

Small, branching shrub from Madagascar with oaklike leaves of metallic blue

682. *Is the indoor oak as good a house plant as I have heard?*

Yes. Grow in general-purpose soil (see 1) kept evenly moist and in a sunny window at 65° to 75°F. Prune every spring to keep the plant a convenient, attractive size.

IRIS

Familiar flower growing all over the world, a few types of which can be grown indoors to bloom in winter and spring

683. *What are the best iris for forcing?*

The fragrant purple reticulata iris and the Dutch iris, notably the blue variety, Wedgewood. Both are bulbous types.

684. *How can I grow iris indoors?*

Plant the bulbs (of the types that can be forced) about 1 inch deep, 6 to a 5-inch pot, and follow forcing directions (see 148-152). If planted in early October, you can have bloom about Christmas.

IXIA

South African plant grown from a corm and producing clusters of bell-shaped flowers in a wide range of colors in early spring

685. *How are ixias grown indoors?*

Plant 1 inch deep in general-purpose soil (see 1) in October or November, water well, and put in a cool, sunny place. Then handle like freesias (see 561-563). If you save the corms from year to year, repot in fresh soil every fall.

686. *Why is the bloom of my ixias so unsatisfactory?*

Very possibly because you are not growing them cool

enough or are watering too much between planting and the time they start making good growth. Low night temperature of 45° to 50°F is particularly important to success with these plants.

JACOBEAN LILY (*Sprekelia formosissima*)

Also called Aztec lily, St. James's lily, and Mexican fire lily, a Latin American bulbous plant with large orchidlike flowers of velvety scarlet in spring and summer

687. *Is the Jacobean lily difficult to grow?*

No. Plant each bulb in the spring in a pot about 2 inches larger in diameter than the bulb. Use general-purpose soil (see 1) and let the neck of the bulb protrude above the surface. Place in a cool (50°F), not too bright room and keep soil barely moist until growth starts. Then expose gradually to sun, and increase watering. Apply fertilizer every two to three weeks.

688. *Why did the bud of my Jacobean lily curl up and die soon after it appeared?*

Lack of humidity is the probable cause. If you cannot create enough humidity in the air, cover the lily with a large mason jar or with polyethylene film until the flowering stem has grown 6 inches or more. From then on, the extra humidity is not needed.

689. *How does one save an Aztec lily bulb?*

After flowering, grow on for a month or more in a bright window. Then gradually withhold water, let the foliage die down, and store the bulb, in its pot, in a cool, dark place for three months or more.

JASMINE (*Jasminum*)

Shrubby or climbing tropical plants with white, pink, or yellow flowers and attractive foliage. For indoor culture, select the fragrant *J. officinale grandiflorum,* with white summer flowers; *J. mesnyi,* with yellow spring flowers, and *J. nudiflorum,* with yellow flowers in late winter and early spring

690. *Can I raise a jasmine in the house?*

Yes, if you can keep it in a south window at about 65°F. With good culture it will bloom beautifully, perfuming the entire house, and will grow to 4 feet or more.

691. *Does jasmine need a lot of moisture?*

A considerable amount. Keep the general-purpose soil (see 1) evenly moist though not soaked, and occasionally put the pot in a pail of water so that the deep roots will get adequate moisture. Spray the plant daily during winter and spring, and apply fertilizer every two to three weeks in this period.

692. *Why did the jasmine I was given lose its leaves in the fall?*

It was a deciduous species. Of those previously mentioned, *J. officinale grandiflorum* and *J. nudiflorum* are deciduous, and there are others. *J. Mesnyi* is one of the evergreens.

JERUSALEM CHERRY (*Solanum pseudo-capsicum*)

Also called Christmas cherry, an old world shrub up to 4 feet but usually much smaller with little red or yellow fruits borne in early winter and lasting several months

693. *Are the fruits of the Jerusalem cherry edible?*

Absolutely not. They are poisonous.

694. *Why did the Jerusalem cherry I was given at Christmas die almost immediately?*

Your house is undoubtedly too hot. This plant will thrive only if kept at 50° to 60°F.

695. *Is there a successful way to handle Jerusalem cherry indoors?*

A cool place is a must (see 694). Give plenty of water and spray the foliage daily to increase humidity. Keep in a sunny window.

696. *What should be done with a Jerusalem cherry after it drops its fruit and leaves in March?*

Cut branches back to two buds and put the plant in good light, but not sun, at 40°F. Water only twice a month. When growth starts again in several months, replace the old top soil with new and move the plant to a cool, sunny window until danger of frost is past. Then put outside in filtered sun and keep watered and fertilized. Bring in in September.

697. *How can Jerusalem cherry be grown from seed?*

Sow seeds in flats in early spring. Shift seedlings into pots of general-purpose soil (see 1) and grow outdoors in a light, protected place during the summer. Bring indoors in fall after the fruits have set.

JOSEPHS-COAT (*Alternanthera*)

Bushy, little Brazilian perennial with colorful variegated leaves, and in one species maroon foliage

698. *Is Josephs-coat a satisfactory house plant?*

Yes. It requires general-purpose soil (see 1); a temperature of about 70°F during the day; sun; even moisture at the roots; good ventilation.

699. *How can I bring out the colors in the foliage of Josephs-coat?*

This plant needs a lot of sun when growing indoors, and when moved outdoors in summer it should also be in the sun (see 82). Many people at this time transplant directly into the garden and use the plants as a bedding or border which is kept low by shearing.

JUSTICIA EXTENSA

Decorative Congolese plant with silver-marked foliage and white, red, or violet flower spikes in fall and winter

700. *How can I make justicia do well indoors?*

Justicia requires high humidity (spray the foliage daily with water) and temperatures of 65°F at night, 75°F in the day. Plant in general-purpose soil (see 1) with a double amount of humus and keep constantly moist. Grow in an east window. After flowering, plants become woody and scraggly, so take cuttings and discard the old plant.

KAEMPFERIA ROSCOEANA

Also called peacock plant, ginger lily, a tropical tuberous plant with handsome, large, bronze-marked leaves and fragrant, white-eyed lavender blooms each lasting a day in summer

701. *How is kaempferia grown?*

Plant tubers in early spring in 4-inch pots filled with general-purpose soil (see 1) with an extra quantity of humus. Keep well watered and at an east window at normal house temperatures, or grow under fluorescent light. Fertilize every two to three weeks. If possible, move outdoors into filtered shade in summer.

702. *How are kaempferias handled in winter?*

When flowering stops in fall, gradually withhold water and let foliage die down. Store tubers in their pots in a cool place until late February, then bring out to light, and water thoroughly.

KALANCHOE

Madagascar succulents of several species, the most common being *K. blossfeldiana,* a small, upright plant with clusters of red flowers, which is widely sold by florists at Christmas and which blooms until May

703. *How is kalanchoe grown?*

Much like other succulents (see 957-965), but it needs a soil with more humus and also more water in summer (but keep on the dry side after it is through flowering in late winter).

704. *Can kalanchoe be carried over from year to year? My second-year plant didn't bloom very well.*

Second-year plants usually do not do too well, although severe cutting back of tops after blooming, fertilizing after a two-month rest period, and a summer on a shaded porch may produce quite a satisfactory display the following December. It is, however, better to grow new plants from seed every year.

705. *How are kalanchoes grown from seed?*

In March, press the fine seeds into sterilized soil or vermiculite and keep moist and in good light but not sun until large enough to transplant into individual pots in standard succulent soil. Grow in a cool, east window in summer (crown rot often sets in if plants are outdoors). From September on, grow in a sunny window at 60°F, the ideal temperature for promoting best growth and flower color.

706. *Why doesn't a kalanchoe growing under electric light bloom?*

Kalanchoe is a short-day plant that will not bloom until the hours of light are decreased in winter. By giving it extra light, you interfere with its normal flowering in December and succeeding winter months.

KANGAROO VINE (*Cissus antarctica*)

Durable, adaptable vine from Australia with long, narrow, shiny leaves

707. *Will a kangaroo vine grow in a living room that is not too bright?*

Yes, it grows in poor light and is not fussy about temperature. Grow in general-purpose soil (see 1), water thoroughly when soil feels dry, and fertilize about once a month. Provide a light lattice or strings for tendrils to cling to, and cut back straggling stems to keep it shapely.

KENILWORTH IVY (*Cymbalaria muralis*)

Also called coliseum ivy, Aaron's beard, or climbing sailor, a small old world climbing ivy, good for hanging baskets, with little blue, white, or pink flowers in summer

708. *Can the Kenilworth ivy I saw in England be grown indoors?*

With ease. This is a very adaptable, lovely little plant. Grow it in a small pot or hanging container in full or partial sun. Use general-purpose soil (see 1) and keep it constantly moist. Provide some humidity.

709. *Is it easier to propagate Kenilworth ivy from cuttings or seeds?*

You can do it either way, but this plant seems to produce an inexhaustible supply of seeds that are easily germinated in moist soil at any time of year. New plants will be flowering within about four months.

KINGS-CROWN (*Jacobinea carnea*)

Bushy Brazilian shrub, 2 feet tall, with large, crowded spikes of out-curving, pink flowers in summer

710. *How can I grow kings-crown?*

Pot in general-purpose soil (see 1). Water regularly. Place in an east or west window. Keep warm (not below 65°F) and give reasonably high humidity.

KOHLERIA

Often incorrectly identified as *Isoloma,* a rhizomatous tropical American gesneriad with white, pink, purple, or orange-red flowers from late summer through winter, depending on the species

711. *How are kohlerias grown?*

Like gloxinias (see 618-647). Use the same soil, provide good light with some sun, maintain high humidity, and do not let temperatures fall below 60°F.

712. *I heard that kohlerias do well in a north window, but I am having no luck with them. Was my informant wrong?*

Kohlerias will grow in poor light but produce little

bloom and become rather leggy. An east window is better, and a southern window is excellent, too, during the winter with a little shading at noon if sun is hot.

713. *How are kohlerias propagated?*

By dividing the rhizomes. After planting the sections, water sparingly until growth starts. Or you can propagate from tip cuttings of new growth.

LACHENALIA (Cape cowslips)

Small South African bulbous plant with clusters of red-and-yellow flowers December through February

714. *How is lachenalia grown?*

Like freesia (see 561-563). Low temperature and plenty of sun are essential to success. Plant in August in 5-inch pots just below the soil surface.

LANTANA (*Lantana camara*)

Tall, tropical American shrub with flat, 2-inch clusters of white, yellow, orange, pink, or red flowers throughout the year

715. *How can I get better, longer bloom from lantana?*

Most of all, provide full sun and plenty of water. Hold temperature at about 65°F if possible. Plant in general-purpose soil (see 1) and fertilize about once a month.

716. *Should I prune the lantana that I have had growing outdoors this summer?*

Cut it back to about half its size, but note that old lantana plants are generally not worth saving. It is better to grow new plants from spring or summer cuttings or from seeds. If you pinch the flower buds off the small plants through the summer, you will have a wonderful display indoors from fall on.

717. *Is there any trick to propagating lantana?*

None. Take 4-inch tip cuttings in spring or summer and root them in a mixture of half sand and half peat moss or directly in a soil mixture of 1 part loam, 1 part humus, and 1 part sand in the pots in which they will grow. Keep in shade and maintain humidity around them with a covering of polyethylene film (see 133).

LEMON (*Citrus limonia*)

Subtropical, evergreen fruit tree with fragrant white flowers in February and summer and fruit in fall and winter

718. *Are indoor lemon trees started from the seeds of market fruits?*

Yes, but they rarely flower or bear fruit. Lemon trees grown indoors are usually dwarf or slow-growing varieties, such as Meyer and ponderosa lemon, which are grown from cuttings.

719. *How can I get good results with a Meyer lemon tree?*

Grow in well drained general-purpose soil (see 1) on a barely heated sun porch in a spot where there is partial sun. Keep the porch well ventilated and at 45° to 55°F at night, 65° to 70°F at the very outside during the day. To thwart scale insects, spray foliage regularly except when the tree is in bloom. Water lightly from October to February, but don't let the soil dry out completely. Keep it moist but not soggy the rest of the time.

720. *Is it desirable to move a lemon tree outdoors in summer?*

Yes, it helps to ripen wood, and encourages setting of fruit along about July.

721. *Why has my lemon tree shed its leaves now that I have brought it in from outside?*

This sometimes happens when a lemon tree is suddenly subjected to a new set of conditions, such as low humidity and high heat. But if you give it the low temperature and care it requires, it should soon develop new leaves.

LEOPARD PLANT (*Ligularia tussilaginea aureo-maculata*)

Also identified as *L. kaempferi aureo-maculata*, a small Japanese plant with large leaves spotted yellow, white, or pink, and yellow flowers in summer

722. *Does a leopard plant require full sun?*

It will grow in any light window, but color is better with some sun, as in an east window, and the temperature should be on the cool side, not above the 60's. Use a general-purpose soil (see 1) and keep it evenly moist.

LILY-OF-THE-VALLEY (*Convallaria majalis*)

Fragrant perennial from the middle South and Eurasia with loose clusters of nodding white flowers in winter and spring

723. *How are lilies-of-the-valley grown indoors?*

The plants grow from small, upright buds attached to wiry roots, called "pips." Plant these in moist sphagnum moss or sand so tips just show above the surface. Store in a 70°F, dark place for seven to ten days. Keep well watered. Then gradually expose to more light and finally set in a sunny window. Flowering should start in about three weeks and will continue for little more than a week, but in that brief time you will enjoy one of the sweetest fragrances known.

724. *I bought some lily-of-the-valley pips for growing indoors, but they grew badly and had almost no flowers. What could I have done wrong?*

You probably bought pips meant for outdoor growing. For indoor flowers, buy only the large pips that have been held in cold storage in preparation for forcing.

LITTLE PICKLES (*Othonna crassifolia*)

Small, trailing South African succulents with tiny picklelike leaves and yellow flowers from December to September

725. *Is the succulent called little pickles easy to grow?*

Give it sun, and warmth (see 957-965). Water when soil feels dry except in early fall, when it is resting and the supply should be reduced.

LIVING STONES (*Lithops*)

Small succulents that resemble rocks divided by a fissure from which white or yellow flowers rise in fall

726. *How can I grow those fascinating plants called living stones?*

Plant in 2 parts loam, 2 parts sand, and 1 part peat moss. To keep the roots cool, sink the pot in sand or gravel. Give full sun in a room about 65°F. Water May to November; thereafter only when the plants look as if they might shrivel.

MADAGASCAR JASMINE (*Stephanotis floribunda*)

Twining tropical vine with leathery leaves and, in summer, fragrant, waxy, white flowers in clusters

727. *Why is the bloom of my Madagascar jasmine so poor?*

Perhaps you did not give it good care in the spring, when it was setting buds. At this time, the temperature should not go below 65°F. Keep the soil constantly moist, though not soaking wet, feed regularly, and provide a sunny southern exposure.

728. *What do I do with Madagascar jasmine in winter?*

Let it rest. Reduce watering, but do not let the soil dry out completely. Reduce the temperature if possible, but don't go below a minimum of 60°F. During this period, the plant also needs somewhat less sun.

MARANTA

One species also called arrowroot; another, prayer plant, both small tropical plants with handsome leaves marked with yellow, white, or red

729. *What kind of soil should be used for marantas?*

General-purpose soil (see 1) with a double quantity of humus. Keep well watered except when the plants are resting in the autumn.

730. *Do marantas need a great deal of sun to bring out the leaf color?*

No, they have good color in east or west windows or even at fully light north windows.

731. *A friend has suggested that my maranta isn't doing well because it is on the sun porch. Could that be so?*

Quite possibly. Marantas need warmth—at least 65°F—more than you find on the average sun porch in winter. They also require very little sun (see 730) and a humid atmosphere, as in the usual kitchen or bathroom. If you can't provide this kind of humidity, spray the foliage daily with water.

732. *Do you recommend trimming back marantas when they get large?*

In the fall, when they start to rest, cut out the oldest leaves if the growth looks scraggly. Toward January, when plants are ready to grow again, the young leaves will fill in rapidly.

MARGUERITE (*Chrysanthemum frutescens*)

Also called Paris daisy, a Canary Island plant up to 3 feet with white or yellow daisy flowers from February to September. This is a fine colorful addition to the window garden and readily available from the florist.

733. *Why does the marguerite plant I was given seem so languid?*

Possibly because you have not given it enough water; it requires quantities. It also does better if the temperature is in the 60's.

734. *Is it better to carry over old marguerite plants from year to year or start new ones?*

Start new ones; old ones get too large. Cuttings can be taken from March to the end of July, but June is usually best. After these are rooted, pot them in progressively larger pots up to the 5- or 6-inch sizes. Use general-purpose soil (see 1).

735. *How often should marguerites be fertilized?*

When new plants are growing vigorously, feed them every two weeks. They should also be kept very well watered:

set them in a bowl or pail of water at least once a week until the soil surface feels moist. This assures that the deep, spreading roots will get all the moisture they require.

MINIATURE HOLLY (*Malpighia coccigera*)

Bushy West Indian shrub to about 3 feet with glossy leaves and dainty pink flowers in spring and summer followed by red fruit

736. *What are the soil and heat requirements of the miniature holly?*

Grow in general-purpose soil (see 1) at 55°F at night to 70°F during the day.

737. *Does miniature holly need much water?*

Let the soil surface dry between waterings; then soak the plant until water comes out the drainage hole or stand it in a bowl of water and let it draw up water for an hour or so until the soil feels damp—always a good practice with shrubs.

738. *How much sun does the miniature holly require?*

Some but not a great deal. Grow in an east or west window and it will do well.

MEXICAN FOXGLOVE (*Allophyton mexicanum*)

Also known as *Tetranema mexicanum,* a tiny plant with clusters of purple winter flowers borne above leathery leaves

739. *How does one grow Mexican foxglove?*

Plant in general-purpose soil (see 1) and keep it constantly moist. Grow at a sunny window at 55° to 70°F with above-average humidity. Move outdoors in the summer into partial sun.

MONSTERA DELICIOSA (Swiss cheese plant)

Also called *Philodendron pertusum*, a tropical American climber with huge leaves cut into deep lobes and perforated with large holes

740. *How is monstera grown best?*

It demands little attention except regular water-spraying or washing of the large leaves. Grow in a fully light north window and provide a stout support, preferably a bark-covered piece of wood.

741. *Does monstera need special soil or a large amount of fertilizer to make such huge growth?*

It grows well in general-purpose soil (see 1), preferably with double the amount of humus, and requires a little fertilizer about once a month.

742. *How should I trim my monstera down to size? It's gigantic.*

You can air-layer it to produce a smaller plant (see 141), or simply cut it off about 12 inches above the soil. It will soon renew itself.

MORNING GLORY (*Ipomoea purpurea*)

Familiar tropical vine that produces delightful white, blue, red, and pink flowers in fall and early winter

743. *When should morning glories be planted for winter bloom?*

In August; they will take about three months to flower. Use general-purpose soil (see 1) with a double quantity of sand. Plant a half dozen or so seeds in the 6-inch pots in which they will grow and later thin to three plants. Give plenty of sun and strings or wire to climb on.

744. *Why don't I get better bloom from morning glories indoors?*

Possibly because the temperature is not right. Good flowering at any time of year occurs when the temperature is 62° to 65°F. If the temperature goes higher, the plants will flower well only when the days are short—from about November through December. If it goes lower, the days must be long.

745. *Is there a trick to making morning glory seeds germinate quickly?*

Soak them in warm water for twenty-four hours before planting or nick the heavy seed coat with a knife.

MOSES-IN-THE-CRADLE (*Rhoeo discolor*)

Tropical American plant with long, densely overlapping leaves and small white flowers in boatlike bracts off and on through the year

746. *Is Moses-in-the-cradle a plant that my small child can take care of?*

Moses-in-the-cradle is indeed child's play. It requires only general-purpose soil (see 1), morning or afternoon sun, even moisture at the roots, normal house temperatures.

MOSS

Numerous small, green, flowerless plants of varying sizes, shapes, and textures

747. *Can I grow indoors moss that I have collected in the woods?*

Mosses are excellent for terrariums and dish gardens and are commonly used as a ground-cover under bonsai. Not all will tolerate home conditions, but the only way to tell which will is to try them. In every case, try to grow your moss indoors under the same conditions (or close to them) that you found outdoors. Most kinds prefer shade, but some require a little sun.

748. *What is the best soil for moss?*

Mosses that you purchase will usually grow satisfactorily in general-purpose soil (see 1) with a double quantity of humus, preferably leaf mold. If you collect mosses from the wild, bring with them a quantity of the soil in which they are growing.

749. *Doesn't moss require a lot of water?*

Yes, but don't overdo it unless the moss comes from a bog. Just keep the soil evenly moist. As a rule, moss grows well in terrariums because of the high humidity.

MYRTLE (*Myrtus communis*)

The true myrtle, a large Mediterranean evergreen shrub with shiny green, aromatic leaves and white or pink flowers in summer followed by purple-black berries

750. *How should I care for the little plant of classic myrtle I was given?*

Grow in a cool, south window or on a cool (under 60°F) sun porch. Pot in general-purpose soil (see 1). Water when the soil feels dry. The foliage can be sheared like boxwood.

NARCISSUS to grow in water

Fragrant daffodils particularly suited to indoor culture that can be brought into bloom from Thanksgiving into the spring. Also see "daffodils" for forcing (476-477)

751. *What are the best narcissus to grow in water?*

Paperwhites—pure white; Soleil d'Or—yellow with orange cups; Chinese sacred lily—white with yellow cups; and Cragford—white with scarlet cups.

752. *How are narcissi planted when they are grown in water?*

Fill a bowl 4 to 5 inches deep to within about 2 inches of the rim with white pebbles. Set the bulbs 1 inch apart and with the upper three-quarters exposed. Keep bowl filled with water so that it just touches the base of the bulbs. They must not be floated. If bulb fiber is used instead of pebbles, plant in the same way and keep fiber moist but not soaking.

753. *When is the right time to start narcissi and how should they be handled?*

Plant from October 15 on. After planting (see 752), set them in a cool, dark spot until growth appears in two to three weeks, then gradually expose to sun. Maintain the water supply throughout the growing and blooming period.

754. *Why should narcissi bloom poorly in our new house? In our old house they did well.*

Perhaps because your new house is warmer than the old. Narcissi do best at 60° to 65°F—never higher than 70°F.

755. *I planted narcissi in a shallow bowl of pebbles. Is it harmful if the roots push the bulbs out of the pebbles?*

No, but it does spoil the effect of your planting. Push them gently back into the pebbles as far as you can, and next time use a deeper bowl (see 752).

756. *Can I save narcissus bulbs that have been growing in water?*

Throw them away. Unlike bulbs grown in soil, they have had no opportunity to renew the strength they lose in producing flowers.

NATAL PLUM (*Carissa grandiflora*)

Bushy South African shrub with spines, glossy foliage, fragrant white flowers throughout much of the year (but primarily in summer) and 1- to 2-inch red fruits

757. *Can the natal plum used as a hedge in the South be grown indoors?*

Yes. Plant in general-purpose soil (see 1), give full sun, a temperature to 70°F during the day, and water regularly. It can be shifted to the garden in summer and brought indoors before frost.

NAUTILOCALYX

Erect South American gesneriad, up to 2 feet, with handsome foliage which hides the small yellow spring flowers

758. *Is nautilocalyx as good a house plant as the other gesneriads?*

Yes, but it is not so showy as many of the others. Grow it like an episcia (see 506-507) in porous soil, a warm temperature, with good light and high humidity.

759. *Why are the lower leaves of my nautilocalyx falling?*

Probably the room is too cool. These gesneriads need 60° to 75°F. Spray the foliage with water every day, if possible.

760. How can I prevent nautilocalyx from looking so sparse?

If you pinch out the center shoots, side shoots will usually develop. This makes a bushier plant which is much better looking.

761. How should I handle nautilocalyx after it blooms?

Cut out the oldest stems. If you do this, the plant can be kept in almost constant growth.

NECKLACE VINE (*Muehlenbeckia complexa*)

Also called wire vine, maidenhair vine, a New Zealand plant with twining, wiry stems, tiny round green leaves, and insignificant white flowers

762. How easy is the necklace vine to grow?

It is one of the least demanding plants, requiring only ordinary soil, regular watering, and considerable sun. It becomes difficult only if the temperature goes much above 75°F or below 55°F. In summer it does well outdoors—so well, in fact, that hard pruning is required before you bring it in.

763. Can necklace vine be used as a trailer?

It makes an attractive trailer and stands considerable pruning. If grown upward, it requires the support of strings or wires to twine around.

NEOREGELIA

Bromeliads with sturdy leaves in a rosette and some with lovely flowers. Excellent foliage varieties are painted fingernail (*N. spectabilis*) and marble plant (*N. marmorata*). Crimson cup (*N. farinosa*) has beautiful red-blue bracts in spring

764. *Is it safe to grow neoregelia in a south window?*

Yes, if it is shaded from midday sun, especially in summer. An east or west window is better.

765. *Why has my neoregelia lost its leaf markings?*

Probably because you are not giving it enough light. This plant needs two to three hours of sun every day. For culture, see 342-353.

NEPHTHYTIS AFZELI

Very adaptable tropical American, rhizomatous climber with arrowhead leaves on long stems

766. *Can nephthytis be grown satisfactorily in a room with little sun?*

Yes, even at light north windows. The plant needs little care as long as it has warmth and moisture. Grow in general-purpose soil (see 1).

767. *Can nephthytis, like philodendron, be grown in water?*

Yes, it does well especially if you give it a little complete plant food incorporating all the trace elements. Let it droop, or provide a piece of bark for it to cling to and grow up on.

NORFOLK ISLAND PINE (*Araucaria excelsa*)

Symmetrical evergreen tree that eventually reaches 10 feet from Norfolk Island in the Pacific Ocean

768. *Does Norfolk Island pine dislike sun? I had a fine plant but after I moved it to a south window it failed.*

This handsome little tree will tolerate some sun but does

better in a north window. In summer, when you move it outside, keep it in light shade.

769. *What does Norfolk Island pine require to do well?*

Mainly a temperature of 60°F or less, good light but no sun, and regular watering. Plant in general-purpose soil (see 1).

770. *Why did the tip cuttings from branches of my Norfolk Island pine produce low shrubs instead of tall, symmetrical trees?*

This is a peculiarity of the tree. To get upright plants, you must remove the leader (top of the trunk) and use the tips of the new leaders that develop for cuttings. But this, of course, ruins the appearance of the original tree. Better leave the propagating of Norfolk Island pines to florists.

OLEANDER (*Nerium oleander*)

Mediterranean shrub up to 8 feet with gorgeous white, pink, red, or purple flowers from mid-spring into the summer. The wood and juices of the plant are poisonous

771. *Is oleander a good house plant?*

It is attractive but large—best for a sun porch, not the living room. Flowering may start indoors about April but reaches its peak after the plant is moved to the sunny terrace in May.

772. *How do I care for oleanders in winter?*

Keep in a cool (down to 50°F at night), sunny place. Water when surface soil dries. Repot or work in fresh soil when growth starts about March; increase water; apply fertilizer. Move outside into full sun when frost danger is past.

773. *How and when are oleanders pruned?*

Cut back about a quarter of the growth when you bring the plants indoors in fall. Flowers are borne on new wood.

ORANGE (*Citrus* of several species)

Subtropical fruit tree with fragrant white flowers about February and in summer and fruit in fall and winter

774. *What are good orange trees to grow indoors?*

The otaheite and calamondin orange, both dwarfs with small, inedible fruit. These are grown from cuttings.

775. *Will an orange tree grown from seed of a store fruit bear fruit, or should I buy plants?*

A tree grown from seed will produce fine foliage but it is not likely to flower; and unless it flowers, it will not bear fruit.

776. *How should I care for the orange tree I was recently given?*

All citrus trees are grown about the same way (see 718-721).

777. *Is it necessary to hand-pollinate an orange tree in order to get fruit?*

No, but it may help. With a cotton swab or artist's paint brush transfer the powdery pollen from one flower to the stigma of another. The stigma should be naturally moist and sticky at the time. (*Illustration 20*)

778. *The foliage of my orange tree is beginning to turn yellow. What should I do?*

Alternately fertilize with an ordinary balanced plant food

and one containing chelated iron. This is available from the best garden supply stores.

779. *What should I do about an orange tree whose leaves are sticky and have brown lumps?*

The stickiness is probably caused by aphids, the lumps by scale insects. Both can be scrubbed off with soapy water and a fairly stiff brush. To prevent future attacks, syringe tops occasionally with water or wipe the leaves with a soft wet cloth.

20. Pollinating an orange tree

ORANGE BROWALLIA (*Streptosolen jamesoni*)

Shrubby South American vine with clusters of orange flowers in winter and spring

780. *How well does orange browallia do in the home?*

Very well. It grows in general-purpose soil (see 1) that is kept moist, and at 55° to 65°F, preferably in a south window, though growth is also good in an east or west exposure.

781. *How can I improve the growth of an orange browallia?*

If it's a young plant, pinch off the shoots several times to encourage branching. If it's an old plant, cut it back about a third after it has flowered (and don't worry about saving old stems because flowers come on new growth). Prune the roots in proportion (see 331-332), repot in fresh soil and grow outdoors until frost in filtered sun.

ORCHIDS

This immense family of beautiful flowers includes a number of good house plants—*Bletilla, Cattleya, Cypripedium, Dendrobium nobile,* reed *Epidendrum, Phaius, Phalaenopsis, Sophronitis coccinea,* and *Vanda*

782. *Which orchids shall I try first in my window garden?*

Bletilla is the most easily grown, because it is handled like any tender bulb (see 801-802). It has such small flowers, however, that you might not think of it as an orchid and it doesn't always bloom year after year. Among the large-flowered types, the reed epidendrums followed by the cattleyas are the easiest (see 806 and 803). Start with a few mature plants that you can buy, grow them properly, and you will soon find yourself a slave to this gorgeous family of flowers.

783. *Which orchids produce sprays of flowers?*

Some that are fairly easy to grow in the house are the dendrobiums that have sprays of lavender, white, yellow, brown, brownish-red flowers in spring or fall; phalaenopsis, with generally white or pinkish-lavender flowers in winter; and the vandas that bear large, fairly flat flowers in almost every color at different times of the year depending on the species.

784. *Do the miniature orchids make better house plants than the large standard types?*

Miniatures require the same care as the large orchids, but are popular as house plants because they take up so much less space yet produce lovely, large flowers.

785. *What are some of the best miniature orchids?*

The orchid family has a number of miniature varieties. Some of the best are among the oncidiums, epidendrums, laelias, and trichocentrums. A particularly delightful plant is sophronitis coccinea, which is only about 3 inches tall and bears bright orange-red flowers almost 3 inches in diameter in fall and winter. It is grown like standard orchids.

786. *What soil do orchids require?*

The epiphytic, or tree-growing, orchids, such as the cattleyas, are potted in osmunda fiber (also called orchid peat) or in chopped bark, a newer material that is much easier to handle. The terrestrials, such as phaius and bletilla, are potted in the various mixtures suggested below for each kind.

787. *How are orchids potted?*

Unless you are an expert, grow plants that have been potted for you. Very briefly, however, you should grow them in red clay orchid pots which have extra drainage holes or drainage slots. Fill pots at least a third full of shards or gravel. Pot the plants tight in osmunda fiber either when root growth starts or right after blooming.

Bletilla is one exception to all this. You can easily pot it up yourself (see 801).

788. *Should orchids be repotted when the roots climb out of the pot?*

No, repotting usually prevents the plants from blooming for a year. The fact that the roots have grown thick outside of the pot is nothing to worry about. This is the way orchids grow. Leave the roots alone and spray the plants often with water.

789. *What fertilizer do orchids need?*

Apply a water-soluble food prepared especially for orchids no more than once a month. Supplement with a little extra nitrogen (see 68) if the plants are potted in chopped bark. But always remember that it is better to underfeed than overfeed orchids.

790. *My orchids have turned yellow-green and look pretty thin. What causes this?*

Probably too much fertilizer. Flush out the soil with water and repot. Do not fertilize more than once a month from now on.

791. *How warm must my house be for orchids?*

Normal indoor day temperatures suit orchids, but night temperatures must fall to 55° to 60°F for about six hours to encourage bud formation.

792. *Don't orchids require more humidity than is normal in a house?*

Orchids need a relative humidity of 50 to 75 per cent, but are harmed by a muggy atmosphere. Keep the pots in a plant tray filled with shards or charcoal lumps which are kept wet just to the surface (they absorb water and give it off slowly). Also spray the plants daily with a fine water mist so long as the water evaporates rapidly. If it doesn't, fungi may attack the plants.

793. *Should orchid roots be kept wet all the time?*

Absolutely not. The osmunda or bark in which they are planted should be allowed to dry out completely between waterings. But when you do water, take the plants to the sink and give each a couple of quarts in order to wash out accumulated salts.

794. *Do orchids prefer sun or shade?*

They will grow in shade but not bloom. For flowering, you must have plenty of sun. In the North, keep plants at a south window through the year, but shade them with cheesecloth from the midday sun during spring and summer. In the South, keep plants at a south window also, but shade them at midday the year round.

795. *What causes big brownish-black spots to form suddenly on orchid leaves?*

Too much sun if the spots are hard. These do no harm, though they are unsightly and will not heal. If the spots are soft and juicy, fungus is to blame. Cut them out with a knife, being sure to go well behind the affected areas, and treat with a fungicide such as Wilson's Anti-Damp.

796. *One of my orchids has shot up pretty tall while another is sending out drooping growth at the sides. Neither blooms well. What is the trouble?*

Lack of sun (see 794). The old idea that orchids would grow only in the shade has been disproved. In the home especially, bright light with plenty of sun is necessary.

797. *In the North, is it safe to move orchids outdoors in summer?*

Yes, provided they are not subjected to freezing; but it

is better to keep them inside until you can be pretty sure the temperature will stay above 60°F. Then to avoid sunburn, move them into deep shade and gradually into partial sun. Their final location should be under a tree that filters out the midday and early afternoon sun or on the east side of the house, where they get morning sun only.

798. *What causes a fungus to develop at the points where I cut orchid flowers?*

You are leaving too much of the flower sheath. This traps moisture, fungus goes to work, and pretty soon, unless you cut out the diseased areas, the plant is killed. When cutting flowers, be sure to cut down the sheath as far as possible.

799. *How do I get rid of the white scale on my orchid?*

With a soft toothbrush, scrub the entire plant thoroughly with soap and water. Or spray three times at two-week intervals with malathion.

800. *What causes small yellowish spots on the surface of orchid leaves along with little rusty indentations underneath?*

Red spider, which is particularly fond of dendrobiums and cymbidiums. Dust with sulfur or a miticide such as malathion.

801. *Should bletilla orchids be planted in osmunda?*

No, this dainty winter-blooming Asiatic orchid with swordlike foliage and small violet flowers is a terrestrial orchid that grows from tuberlike bulbs. Plant these just below the surface of general-purpose soil (see 1) and keep evenly moist. Place in an east window and fertilize about every three weeks. Flowering starts in two months.

802. *How should bletilla be handled after it blooms?*

Keep the foliage growing. Plunge the pots in the garden in partial shade after the weather is warm. Keep well watered. In fall, after foliage dies down, move to a cool dark place indoors; withhold water. Rest the plant for about two months. Then bring it to the light and start to water again. Give some fertilizer at this time.

803. *When can I expect flowers from the mature cattleya plant I was given?*

Not until it has developed into a thickened, club-shaped stem with one or two leaves and a bud sheath. This will take a number of months, depending on the variety. The spectacular purple flower that has made this epiphytic orchid the florist's favorite will appear from the base of the leaves. When growing well, the bloom of cattleyas extends from October to June.

804. *How easy are cypripediums to grow?*

This very beautiful orchid with lady-slipper flowers in many unusual color combinations in winter and spring is one of the easiest. It does not require quite so much sun as most others and is not so fussy about overwatering. However, it does need a night temperature of 70°F.

805. *How are dendrobium nobile orchids cared for?*

These epiphytes require a little more sun than most orchids and must be pot-bound to bloom; otherwise, follow the general culture (see 786-800).

806. *Is there an advantage to planting reed epidendrums in the small wooden cribs that some people use?*

These four-sided orchid baskets are often used for epiphytic orchids such as the almost ever-blooming reed epidendrums with their huge clusters of multi-colored flowers. Many fanciers prefer them to clay pots because they aerate the roots better, assure perfect drainage, and are attractive. However, it is difficult to water them without making a mess in your home. Much simpler, less expensive, but very good containers can be made out of round plastic ice cream cartons with a couple of large V-shaped notches cut along the bottom edges for drainage.

807. Is the phaius orchid treated like most other orchids?

If they are epiphytic species of the phaius orchid, yes; follow general orchid culture (see 786-800). But if they are terrestrial species, plant in a mixture of sandy loam, humus or osmunda fiber, and rotted manure in equal parts. Grow like an amaryllis (see 225-226). Keep soil moist but not wet. Fertilize every other week when buds are forming. The large cattleyalike flowers, which are mainly brown and white with a lavender lip, appear in the spring. During the summer, set plants outdoors in semishade.

808. Is the phalaenopsis orchid easy to grow indoors?

Follow general orchid culture (see 786-800) but give somewhat less sun and more humidity and 70°F night temperature. Do not disturb the roots; repotting is rarely called for. The plant grows well in osmunda fiber or charcoal lumps. If charcoal is used, the pots should be immersed in water for about three hours every time that water is needed; otherwise the charcoal will not soak up enough moisture.

809. Can vanda orchids be grown indoors like cattleyas?

Follow the same rules (see 786-800), but give a bit more fertilizer and grow in an unshaded south window. You can pot vandas in lump charcoal like phalaenopsis if you wish (see 808).

OXALIS

South American and South African bulbous plants with clover leaves and an abundance of white, pink, red, or yellow flowers in winter. Often used in hanging baskets

810. *When should oxalis bulbs be planted?*

In early autumn, six bulbs to a 6-inch pot. Use general-purpose soil (see 1) and be sure drainage is good. Set bulbs an inch below the surface. Water sparingly until growth appears, then more generously so that the soil is always damp.

811. *Why do I get such poor results with oxalis at an east window where the temperature is not high?*

Oxalis needs the full sun of a south window and must be grown at about 60°F.

812. *Can oxalis bulbs be used a second season?*

After flowering, gradually withhold water and let the growth die down. Then store the bulbs in the pots in dry soil. Start into growth again in September by watering and bringing to a sunny window.

PALMS

Various trees with feathery or fanlike leaves—excellent for churches and rooms that are not very sunny. Two of the most attractive are the kentia palm (*Howea forsteriana*) and the pygmy date palm (*Phoenix roebelini*)

813. *What care does a potted palm demand?*

Plant in general-purpose soil (see 1) and keep it damp

but not wet. Grow in good light but little sun at a temperature of about 65°F or a little lower. When roots fill the pot and the plant is growing actively from April to November, fertilize with liquid plant food every three weeks.

814. *Should I repot my palm often?*

No, palms grow best when slightly pot-bound. Keep in small pots (7-inches is a good size even for 4-foot plants) and repot only every other year about March. Give fresh soil and use only the next size larger pot.

815. *Why has my palm tree turned yellow?*

Possibly because you are not watering it enough. Just pouring on a cupful of water once or twice a week is inadequate. To make sure that deep roots get enough moisture during plant's growing period, put pot in a pail of water every week and let it soak up water until soil surface is damp. Only during winter rest periods is it safe to reduce water supply.

816. *Can I grow palms from the seeds in dates?*

Yes. Plant ½ inch deep in a soil mixture of equal parts loam, humus, and sand. Keep moist and grow at about 70°F. With few exceptions seedlings and small plants are not very attractive and it will be several years before you want to show them off.

817. *Are palms subject to insect attack?*

Aphids and mealy bugs like them. Both can be kept down by spraying the foliage every week with water. If the insects get out of control, spray with malathion.

818. *How can I control scale on potted palms?*

If you spray or wipe the foliage with water every week,

you will discourage this sucking insect. But if an infestation becomes established, you will have to spray with malathion or rub off the pests with a soapy cloth (see 112).

819. *Is the kentia palm a good house plant?*

This familiar florist's palm with graceful curving leaves does very well in the house and looks nice on the porch or covered terrace in the summer. Just be careful not to overfeed, and spray or sponge the leaves frequently to ward off insects.

820. *How is kentia palm repotted when it outgrows its container?*

Unless you want the palm to grow larger, repot in the same size pot in March. Remove the root-ball from the old pot, knock off excess soil, and prune the roots back about a quarter. Then repot in fresh soil.

821. *How do I grow the pygmy date palm?*

Like other palms (see 813-818). This 4-foot feather palm with graceful, drooping foliage is an attractive, amenable house plant so long as you don't keep the soil too wet. And don't fertilize it too heavily in an attempt to hurry its growth, because it develops slowly and will react badly to pressure.

PANDANUS (Screw pine)

Shrub from the South Pacific with very long, narrow leaves banded with white or silver

822. *How much care does a screw pine demand?*

You can't neglect it; on the other hand, you don't have to hover over it. Grow in general-purpose soil (see 1) at an east or west window at 65° to 75°F. Water regularly from January to September, but reduce the supply slightly in the last months of the year.

823. *My pandanus seems to be pot-bound. Should I repot it?*

Not necessarily. Fertilize it occasionally and it should grow better. Wait to repot until it begins to push itself well out of the pot. Then replant it in fresh soil in the next size larger pot.

824. *Can the suckers of a pandanus be propagated?*

Cut off the suckers in spring and root them in sand or sandy soil.

PASSION FLOWER (*Passiflora*)

Tropical American vine with large, beautiful, intricate, flowers mainly purple and white that bloom for a day in spring and summer

825. *What is proper winter care for the passion flower?*

Cut it back in the fall when you bring it indoors. Grow in a sunny window and provide support for the tendrils to climb on. When active growth starts in late winter, repot if necessary. Water and fertilize regularly.

826. *Shouldn't a passion flower plant bloom in winter?*

It starts developing buds in late winter, but blooms in spring and summer. Do not try to hurry it. In early winter, when the plant wants to rest, keep it fairly dry and in a cool place. In late winter, as growth starts, increase temperature and water.

827. *Should a passion flower plant be moved outdoors in warm weather?*

If possible, yes. It gets pretty big for the house. Plunge the pot in a somewhat sunny location (see 82) near a fence or trellis that it can grow on.

828. *If I make cuttings of a passion flower in summer, will I have blooming plants by spring?*

Yes. Take cuttings in late summer or early fall and root them in a tumbler of water or moist sand. Then move to 3-inch pots of general-purpose soil (see 1).

PATIENCE (*Impatiens*)

Upright, 2- to 3-foot plant from many parts of the world with small, flat, almost constant pink, red, or white flowers

829. *Patience grows beautifully outdoors in shade; will it do as well indoors?*

No, it needs sun in the house and plenty of moisture, although the soil should not be kept soaking wet. It is one of the best flowering house plants.

830. *If I cut back a patience plant that has grown too big, will it come back?*

Yes, but it is unlikely to be a very good looking plant. Better start new plants every year. Sow seeds outdoors in May or June or take cuttings a little later. Pot and grow the small plants outside in shade and bring in early in fall.

831. *I bought a packet of patience seeds thinking they would produce only pink flowers, but I got a mixture of colors. Is this normal?*

It is likely to happen. To get a particular variety or color, propagate from cuttings of a favorite plant, not from seeds (see 130-133).

832. *The patience I used to grow made big plants over 2 feet. Why are my present plants so much smaller?*

Probably you have planted a different species. The big plants were undoubtedly *I. holsti;* the small one, *I. sultani.* Both of these are excellent, but they have been crossed to produce some even lovelier hybrids.

PELLIONIA

Tropical Asian trailing plant with interesting variegated leaves

833. *Can pellionia be grown as well in a house as a greenhouse?*

Only if you can provide fairly high humidity (see 92), 65° to 75°F warmth, and plenty of water at the roots. Grow in a bright window but with little sun.

834. *How should I grow pellionia?*

In a hanging basket or as a creeper in a large planter or as a climber on a rough, bark-covered piece of wood.

PENTAS LANCEOLATA (Egyptian star cluster)

Small, bushy Arabian plant with tight clusters of tubular pink, red, or white flowers in early fall

835. *How is pentas grown?*

From February to October, grow at 60° to 65°F night temperature (10 degrees higher during the day) in a south window. Water regularly, especially in spring and summer, fertilize every two weeks, and mist the foliage in summer. Grow outdoors in sun in warm weather and bring in before frost. Flowering occurs both outdoors and in. From November through January, grow at 55° to 60° night temperature; do not overwater but mist tops occasionally. Repot in fresh soil before starting into growth again.

836. *How is pentas propagated?*

Make cuttings of half-ripe wood in late winter or early spring. Keep moist and shaded until roots form. Then move to 3-inch pots of general-purpose soil (see 1).

PEPEROMIA

One species also called watermelon begonia; a South American tropical, stemless plant with fleshy, heart-shaped leaves with silver or cream-colored markings

837. *What culture do peperomias require? I never have much luck with them.*

Given proper conditions, peperomias are easy to grow in a warm, fully light north window with plenty of humidity to promote luxuriant growth. Provide a general-purpose soil (see 1) with extra humus and keep it damp but not soggy.

838. *What causes the brownish-lined spots on the leaves of one of my peperomias?*

Probably a virus. Destroy the plant. Sucking insects also attack peperomia leaves underneath but they can be washed off or sprayed away with malathion.

839. *Can I propagate peperomias from leaf cuttings?*

Yes, this is another plant that can be started in this fascinating way (see 140). You can also propagate it from stem cuttings.

PEPPER (*Capsicum frutescens*)

South American plant with small, red, purple, or cream-colored fruits, particularly popular at Christmas

840. How can a gift pepper plant be made to last longer in the house?

Grow in a sunny window but maintain a temperature no higher than 60°F. Water regularly from the top and once a week set the pot in a bowl of water to take in moisture from below. Spray the foliage with water when you do this.

841. Can I grow ornamental peppers myself?

Certainly. Sow seeds in pots or flats outdoors in June or July. When seedlings are well leafed out, transplant to individual 4-inch pots of general-purpose soil (see 1). Set in full sun and don't let the soil dry out. Bring in before frost and keep in a cool, sunny window. No further repotting is necessary.

PERISTROPHE ANGUSTIFOLIA AUREO-VARIEGATA

A more or less trailing plant from Java with soft green and gold leaves and pink flowers from winter through summer

842. What are the requirements of peristrophe?

General-purpose soil (see 1); normal house temperature —up to 80°F; evenly moist soil; reasonably high humidity—set the pot on wet pebbles (see 92).

843. Is full sun essential to peristrophe?

No. Good light with a little sun is satisfactory, but this plant does very well in a south window.

PHILODENDRON

Ever-popular, reliable, climbing or trailing vine from tropical America with handsome foliage in various sizes and shapes

844. *How can I get luxuriant growth in a philodendron? Mine stays alive but that is about all.*

Philodendron needs more light (though not necessarily sunlight) than some people give it, and it also needs a reasonably humid atmosphere. Spray the leaves with water once a week or oftener. Grow at 60° to 70°F and give a plant tablet once a month.

845. *Why doesn't the philodendron I grow in water do better? Would feeding help?*

Philodendron grows quite well in water but much better in soil because it has nourishment there. Feeding a water-grown plant helps some if you use a complete plant food that includes the essential trace elements (see 72).

846. *Why do the lower leaves of my philodendron dry out? I water it every day.*

You are probably drowning the plant—giving it so much water that the roots do not receive or absorb the oxygen they need. Repot in fresh, porous, well-drained soil, and water thoroughly only when surface becomes almost dry.

847. *Why are the leaves of my philodendron getting smaller and smaller and farther apart on the stems?*

Too little light, too little warmth, too little humidity, and lack of nutrients in the soil result in such poor growth. Overwatering may also cause this condition.

848. *Could I improve a straggly philodendron by pinching out the ends of the shoots?*

Yes, this will force branching; but you should also improve the conditions under which the plant is growing (see 844).

849. *Should a philodendron be repotted often?*

Usually only every two or three years, because the root system is not large. When you do repot, work in as much fresh general-purpose soil (see 1) as possible.

850. *Do you advise syringing the foliage of philodendrons?*

Yes. It keeps leaves clean and the plant in good health. No house plant does its best if the foliage is covered with dust.

851. *The leaves of my split-leaved philodendron are not splitting any more. What is wrong?*

Perhaps you are not growing the plant in good enough light or the soil is kept soggy. Or perhaps the plant needs more fertilizer. Philodendron, it seems, goes on and on without fertilizer; but a light monthly feeding—especially for the large-leaved varieties—is most beneficial.

852. *The roots of my big-leaved philodendron have grown out of the pot and are sprawling all over the place. Can they be cut back?*

Untangle them as much as possible but don't try to loosen those that are firmly embedded in the soil. Prune back some of them to about 6 inches and stick the ends in the soil. Cover with more soil.

853. *Are the big-leaved philodendrons propagated in water like the little varieties?*

You will be more successful if you root the cuttings in a moist mixture of sand and peat moss. You can also air-layer the plants (see 141).

PICK-A-BACK PLANT (*Tolmiea menziesi*)

Low-growing North American foliage plant with hairy leaves from the base of which many little plants grow

854. *What light and warmth does the pick-a-back plant need?*

Grow in an east or west window at about 65°F and keep the soil evenly moist but not soggy. This pleasant little plant is easy to care for.

855. *Is there a special technique for propagating pick-a-back plants from the plantlets on the leaves?*

Cut off the leaves on which the plantlets grow, lay them on moist sand, and peg or weight down. If you leave a bit of stem on each leaf, insert this in the sand up to the base of the leaf. Either way, the plantlets will soon put down roots. Another way to propagate this plant is to suspend leaves, with plantlets attached, over water so the water just touches the leaf stems. After plantlets are rooted, pot them up in general-purpose soil (see 1).

PILEA

Family of tropical American plants grown for their foliage, which varies widely among species. Common names given to different species include aluminum plant, artillery plant, friendship plant, panamiga

856. *Is the aluminum plant a good one for terrariums?*

Yes, it thrives in a moist atmosphere but also grows well in pots. Plant in general-purpose soil (see 1) and keep well watered at an east window.

PINEAPPLE (*Ananas*)

Familiar fruit grown indoors as a foliage plant, a bromeliad

857. *How can I start a pineapple plant indoors?*

Cut through the flesh of the fruit just below the leaves. Allow the cut to dry twenty-four hours and sprinkle with a root hormone to speed up growth. Set in damp sand or sandy soil in a dark place for about five weeks until roots develop. Then move into a large pot with a deep layer of drainage material and a humusy soil. (*Illustration 21*)

21. How to grow a pineapple

858. *Where shall we grow a pineapple plant our small daughter has started?*

Put it in a warm, sunny window and do not overwater—a very wet soil is death to this plant. Feed every two to three weeks.

PITCHER PLANT (*Sarracenia flava*)

Also called trumpets, trumpet-leaf, green regent, an insectivorous plant from the eastern United States with tall, pitcher-shaped yellow-green leaves with red throats in spring and sometimes again in fall. Solitary yellow flowers appear at the same time

859. *How do pitcher plants catch insects?*

The insects are lured by nectar into the pitcher-shaped leaves. Once inside, they are prevented from coming out by stiff bristles, so they proceed on down and fall into an acid pool that digests them.

860. *How often should I water my pitcher plant?*

This bog plant needs considerable moisture but never alkaline water. If you are in doubt about your water supply, better save rain water. Grow in an east or southeast window.

861. *Do pitcher plants need fertilizer?*

Like other insectivorous plants, pitcher plants do not need food of any kind. They should be planted in peat moss or sphagnum mixed with a little sand.

PITTOSPORUM TOBIRA

Slow-growing Australasian shrub up to 6 feet with leathery,

dark green leaves and clusters of fragrant white flowers in winter

862. Can I grow pittosporum easily indoors?

Yes, if you can provide a cool (45° to 55°F) south window for it. Plant in general-purpose soil (see 1) and water well when the soil feels dry. Small pittosporum plants do well in a terrarium.

POINSETTIA

Tropical American Christmas plant with enormous red, pink, or white bracts commonly considered to be the flowers

863. How can I make my Christmas poinsettia last longer?

Place at a light but not sunny window at a day temperature of 65°F and a night temperature no lower than 60°F. Avoid drafty locations and hot radiators. Keep soil evenly moist, never soggy. Remove fancy wrappings from the pot and set the pot in a pebble-filled saucer (see 92) to provide necessary humidity. With this care, your plant should not begin to lose its leaves until February.

864. How can I get my gift poinsettia to bloom another year?

Gradually reduce water after blooming ends, and when leaves turn yellow, stop entirely. Store the plant in a basement or garage where the temperature is 50° to 60°F. In early May, cut the top down to 6 inches, repot in fresh soil in the same container, bring to a sunny, 65°F window, and start watering. Move outdoors when the weather is warm and plunge the pot in a sunny location. Continue watering and fertilize about every three weeks. In August, prune the plant back a third and cut out all but three or five stems, depending on the size of the plant. Bring indoors again about September 1 and set in a sunny, cool window. Feed every two weeks from November on.

865. *Is it better to try to carry over an old poinsettia or take cuttings from it and start new plants?*

You will probably get better results from new plants. In spring, when you bring the old plant up from the basement and cut it back (see 864), get it growing vigorously. Then take tip cuttings when the new growth is about 5 inches high and start these in moist sand under polyethylene film (see 133). When these are rooted, transfer to 3-inch pots of general-purpose soil (see 1). Grow outdoors in a fairly sunny place during the summer and keep watered and fertilized. Repot in larger containers as the plants develop. Bring indoors in September.

866. *When I move old poinsettias outdoors in summer, can't I plant them directly in the garden?*

If you do this, they will develop tremendous roots; then when you pot them in the late summer before bringing indoors, you will undoubtedly injure the roots and set the plants back. Poinsettias, like other house plants, are better summered in pots. But repot them in the spring after their winter dormant period (see 864).

867. *The poinsettia I carried over last year was beautiful when I brought it into the living room in September and it stayed healthy. But why didn't it bloom?*

You probably gave it more hours of light than it required. Poinsettias are short-day plants. To bloom, they must have twelve hours of *unbroken* darkness every day from about October 10 on. In other words, keep them in a room in which the lights are not turned on—even for an instant—after the sun sets.

POMEGRANATE (*Punica granatum*)

Small Asiatic shrub with shiny leaves, large orange-red flowers off and on throughout the year and sometimes reddish fruits

868. *How do I handle a pomegranate?*

Give full sun and a cool place (50° to 65°F). Grow in general-purpose soil (see 1) and keep constantly moist except in winter, when the water supply should be reduced as growth slows down. Move outdoors in summer.

869. *Shouldn't I get fruit on my pomegranate?*

If you take care of it, yes. But note that the dwarf, single-flowered variety, *P. nana*, is more likely to fruit than the double-flowered variety.

POTHOS (*Scindapsus*)

Also known as ivy arum. Large plant from the East Indies with leaves marked white, cream, or dark green, grown as a climber or trailer

870. *What care does pothos require?*

Grow it in general-purpose soil (see 1) with an extra quantity of humus. Mix in some charcoal if the container does not have bottom drainage. Water thoroughly when the soil feels dry. Give the plant an unbarked or rough wood stake to grow on (it climbs by aerial roots).

871. *What might be the reason my pothos seems to stand still though it looks healthy?*

Possibly it needs more humidity—some species are more demanding on this score than others—or more fertilizer. You don't have to feed often, but an occasional dose of nourishment will often make a slow plant pick up.

872. *The leaves of my pothos are not as brightly spotted as they should be. How can the variegation be improved?*

Is the plant getting some sun? Pothos doesn't need it just to grow, but if it gets sun several hours a day, the variegation of the leaves is more pronounced. Put it in an east or west window at 60° to 70°F.

873. *Can pothos be grown in water only?*

Yes, but it does better in soil because it gets more nourishment.

874. *How can I improve a pothos that has become bare around the base?*

Pinch back the tops of one or two shoots. This will encourage the lower leaf buds to grow.

PRIMROSE (*Primula*)

Small perennial from many parts of the world with charming, often very delicate flowers in pink, purple, and white in late winter and spring—one of the florist's most delightful flowering plants

875. *Can all primroses be grown indoors?*

No. The best species for indoors are *P. obconica, P. malacoides erikssoni,* and *P. sinensis.*

876. *How much light and water do primroses need?*

Grow in the partial sun of an east window. Keep soil moist but not soggy. Do not get water on the leaves of *P. sinensis.*

877. *How exacting are primroses about temperature?*

They should be grown quite cool—around 50° to 55°F at night.

878. *What would cause my primrose to decay?*

Probably you planted it too low and water stood in the crown. Always plant primroses with the crowns rising a little above the soil level and the soil sloping away from the crown.

879. *Can I carry over an old primrose plant from one year to the next?*

Don't bother. Start new plants each year from seed (see 880) or buy some in full bud from the florist.

880. *How are primroses raised?*

Start with seed sown in January in a moist mixture of sand and peat moss. Keep cool (about 60°F). As the seedlings develop, pot into larger containers (a 5-inch pot is about the largest you will need when a plant is full grown). Use a general-purpose soil (see 1). In summer, keep young plants outdoors in the coolest place possible, in partial shade. Bring indoors in the fall before frost.

881. *Aren't primroses poisonous to the skin?*

P. obconica gives some people—but not all—a rash similar to that of poison ivy.

PSEUDERANTHEMUM

South Pacific shrub up to about 3 feet with variously colored leaves and some with white or purple flowers in winter

882. *How can I get good results with pseuderanthemum?*

Plant in general-purpose soil (see 1) and keep it evenly

moist. Spray the foliage with water once a week. Maintain a 65° to 75°F temperature because this plant suffers from chilling.

883. *Does the coloring of the pseuderanthemum foliage depend on sunlight?*

No. This plant does well in full light with just a little sun —an east or west window, for example.

RANUNCULUS (turban flower)

Tuberous plant from Asia Minor producing yellow, orange, pink, red, or white flowers in October and through the winter if grown from seed

884. *How is ranunculus grown?*

From small tubers planted three to a 6-inch pot in September or from seed sown outdoors in May, the potted seedlings grown on through the summer. Seed sowing is generally safer because field-grown tubers are sometimes diseased. Use a general-purpose soil (see 1) and sterilize it (see 17).

885. *Why do I have such miserable luck with ranunculus?*

Most indoor gardeners have difficulty because this plant requires cold nights—40° to 50°F.

886. *Does ranunculus need a great deal of sun?*

Yes, grow in a cool south window or on a cool, sunny sunporch.

887. *How often should I water ranunculus?*

Keep the soil uniformly moist. Wick-watering (see 60) is good since it helps to solve the problem of crown rot (see 888).

888. *How can I prevent crown rot in ranunculus?*

Grow in sterile soil. Water pots only from the bottom in order not to wet crowns.

RECHSTEINERIA

Compact, tuberous, Brazilian gesneriad with velvety leaves and tubular red or orange flowers in winter, spring, and summer, depending on species and time of planting. One species, *R. leucotricha,* is also known as Brazilian edelweiss

889. *What are the requirements of rechsteineria?*

Much the same as gloxinia's: general-purpose soil (see 1) with extra humus; plenty of sun, but shade at midday in summer; temperature not below 60°F; moderate watering during winter and spring growing period—but let the soil dry out a little between waterings.

890. *When does Brazilian edelweiss bloom and how is it handled after that?*

In June. After blooming, gradually withhold water. When growth dies down completely, handle the tuber as you would a gloxinia (see 634). Start into growth again in December or January.

RED IVY (*Hemigraphis colorata*)

Trailing tropical Asian plant with reddish-purple leaves in the sun, silver in the shade, and insignificant white flowers

891. *How is red ivy raised?*

Pot in general-purpose soil (see 1) and keep it evenly moist. Grow in any bright light (see 892) at 65° to 75°F. Provide high humidity by standing pots in wet pebbles (see 92) and supplement this by frequent spraying with water.

892. *Does the amount of sun affect the color of the red ivy's foliage?*

Yes. If you grow the plant in a fully light north window, the leaves will be silver colored, while in an east or west window they become a lovely reddish-purple.

REDWOOD BURL

A knot or growth from a redwood tree (*Sequoia sempervirens*) that produces green fern-like sprouts when placed in water

893. *How do I handle a redwood burl to get attractive growth?*

Just set it barkside up in a shallow bowl of water and keep in a good light, such as a north window. It will soon start putting out its delicate "fronds." They will last for months as long as you maintain the water supply.

RHEKTOPHYLLUM MIRABILE

Also identified as *Nephthytis picturata,* a climbing Congolese foliage plant with arrow-shaped, papery leaves marked with silver and up to 3 feet long

894. *Can I grow rhektophyllum in the house?*

Indeed yes, it is adaptable and attractive. Plant in general-purpose soil (see 1) kept evenly moist and set in an east or west window. Normal house temperatures satisfy the plant, but humidity should be high, so spray the leaves with water several times a week.

895. *What support does the delightful rhektophyllum need?*

This plant produces aerial roots, so it clings readily to a

rough piece of wood—bark-covered, for the sake of appearance—and climbs. It will easily go up 6 feet.

ROSARY VINE (*Ceropegia woodi*)

Also known as string of hearts, a delicate, graceful succulent vine from Natal with small, thick, heart-shaped leaves marbled with silver and inconspicuous purple flowers in summer

896. *Is the rosary vine adaptable to home conditions?*

A very good house plant, it does not require much sun although it grows well in a south window and at normal house temperatures. Water only when the soil feels dry to the touch.

897. *Is general-purpose soil mixture satisfactory for the rosary vine?*

Yes, provided the loam you use is not too heavy. Rosary vine needs a porous soil, so add a little extra sand and humus to the mixture (see 1). To assure good drainage, put a ½-inch layer of shards in the pot (see 24-25).

898. *Is my rosary vine dying or is it normal for it to wilt?*

Don't worry about wilting if the vine has been thrifty in the past. Some vines rest briefly and show it by what you might call wilting; others seem to grow the year round. Keep your plant on the dry side until it shows signs of starting into growth again.

899. *Can I propagate the rosary vine from the little tubers on the long stems?*

You can reproduce the plant from the stem tubers or the tuberous roots, and also from the stem cuttings.

ROSE, MINIATURE (*Rosa*)

Tiny plants less than 1 foot high with perfect little rose buds and flowers in white, pink, red, and yellow from January on

900. *What are some good miniature rose varieties?*

Dwarfking, Tom Thumb, and Red Imp—reds; Sweet Fairy, Opal Jewel, and Rosa Rouletti—pinks; Baby Masquerade—yellow; Twinkles—white.

901. *How can I make miniature roses do better indoors?*

They need the full sun of a south window, and if you can't provide this, you should grow them under fluorescent lights placed about 6 inches above the plants. They also need plenty of moisture at the roots and therefore thrive in wick-fed pots (see 60). Spray the leaves daily with water or keep pots on wet pebbles (see 92). Ventilate the room regularly. Dust or spray occasionally with an all-purpose insecticide-fungicide.

902. *How often should I fertilize miniature roses indoors?*

Once a month. Use about a teaspoonful of dried rose food or any good liquid plant food.

903. *Should I move miniature roses given me as gift plants outdoors in summer?*

Yes, move them out when the weather moderates and plunge in a sunny location (see 82). Keep watered and fertilized and spray or dust every week to control insects and fungous diseases. Bring indoors before frost.

904. *Should I keep miniature roses in the tiny pots they came in?*

No. Miniature roses have extensive root systems and, like

standard roses which need wide, deep planting holes, they need big, deep pots. So transplant directly into 5- or 6-inch standard pots and spread out the roots in general-purpose soil (see 1) enriched with a little dried manure or bonemeal. This violates the basic rule for repotting house plants (see 47), but after a brief adjustment period, the plants will take hold and revel in the extra root-room you have given them.

ROSEMARY (*Rosemarinus officinalis*)

Tall, erect, branching Mediterranean herb with scented leaves and light blue flowers in spring

905. *Does rosemary grow well indoors?*

Yes, if you meet its simple demands. Plant in general-purpose soil (see 1) and water whenever the soil feels dry. Grow at a south window at a cool temperature (see 906).

906. *Why does my rosemary plant look tired and dry even though I water it regularly?*

Perhaps your home is too warm. Rosemary is not demanding, but it does not do well in a hot room. A temperature in the low 60's is better.

RUBBER PLANT (*Ficus elastica*)

Tree from Malaya with long, glossy leaves sometimes white-marked

907. *How do you get best results from a rubber plant?*

It needs only routine care. Grow in subdued light in general-purpose soil (see 1). Keep soil moist and occasionally set pot in a pail of water so the deep roots can be satisfied. Sponge foliage every couple of weeks with water to keep it clean and shining.

908. *Why has my rubber plant lost its lower leaves?*

As these plants grow older, they are inclined to lose some of their leaves. But your problem might also be the result of poor culture (see 907).

909. *Can I cut back a rubber plant that has become too big?*

You may kill it. Air-layer the main stem (see 141), and when new roots are formed, cut off the new plant and pot it.

910. *Is it a good idea to polish a rubber plant's leaves with oil?*

No. Oil stops up the pores of leaves and slows growth. It can even kill the plant. A healthy rubber plant's foliage will shine without oiling. This is also true of other large-leaved foliage plants.

RUELLIA MAKOYANA (trailing velvet plant)

Trailing Brazilian plant with soft, white-veined leaves and tubular pink flowers in winter

911. *How do I grow the trailing velvet plant?*

Pot in general-purpose soil (see 1) with extra humus. Place at an east window and provide high humidity (see 92). Water regularly to keep the soil evenly moist. Don't let temperature drop below 65°F.

SANCHEZIA NOBILIS GLAUCOPHYLLA

Ecuadorean shrub up to 5 feet with foot-long, lance-shaped leaves veined yellow and clusters of cup-shaped yellow flowers in winter

912. *Is sanchezia a good house plant?*

It does better in a greenhouse where it has a more humid

atmosphere and a fairly high temperature, but if you can meet these two requirements, you should have success with it. Grow in general-purpose soil (see 1) and keep constantly moist. Set in an east window where it will get full light and some sun.

SCILLA (squill)

Spring bulb from Eurasia with clusters of bell-shaped blue, pink, or white flowers

913. *What are good scillas for forcing?*

The early-flowering *Scilla sibirica* is the best.

914. *How can I force scillas for indoor bloom?*

Follow general directions for forcing spring bulbs (see 148-152). Plant in general-purpose soil (see 1) about 1 inch apart, water well, and store in a cold basement or garage until roots are well developed and the pot can be brought into the house.

SEDUM (stonecrop)

Large family of small succulents found mostly in the Northern Hemisphere, many trailing, some upright, some rosette-shaped, some with nice yellow, pink, or red flowers in spring or summer. A familiar favorite is called donkey's tail—fine for hanging baskets

915. *Are sedums satisfactory indoors?*

They grow well if given maximum sun and kept fairly moist in a 60° to 65°F place. Provide general-purpose soil (see 1) with an extra amount of sand. For more on their cultivation, see 957-965.

SENSITIVE PLANT (*Mimosa pudica*)

Tropical American plant with small leaves which fold up when touched

916. *Can I grow sensitive plant indoors?*

A perennial, this is best treated as an annual indoors. Sow seeds in late winter in flats or pots and transplant to larger pots (ultimate size, about 4 inches) in general-purpose soil (see 1) as plants grow. Put in a sunny window at 65° to 70°F, keep soil moist, and provide high humidity (see 92).

SERISSA FOETIDA VARIEGATA

Japanese shrub up to 2 feet with oval, boxwoodlike leaves edged with white and clusters of tiny white flowers in summer

917. *Is serissa a nice plant for the home?*

It is a very pleasant little plant requiring simple culture. Grow in general-purpose soil (see 1) in normal house temperature at a bright but not necessarily sunny light. Keep the soil evenly moist.

918. *Is it true that serissa has an evil odor?*

Apparently some people think the odor worse than others, who don't mind it a bit. In any event, it is noticeable only when the foliage is bruised.

SHRIMP PLANT (*Beloperone guttata*)

Bushy tropical plant with long, pendulous, salmon-pink flowers in winter and through much of the year that do suggest shrimps. Small purple-spotted white flowers hang beneath the bracts but the general effect is shrimp colored

919. *I have been watering my shrimp plant every other day, but it looks peaked. What is wrong?*

Probably too much water. Moisture (as well as sun) is needed, but not a continuously wet soil. Water only when the soil feels dry, and then so thoroughly that an excess runs into the saucer. But do not let the pots stand in this.

920. *Will my shrimp plant do better if I give it a richer soil?*

General-purpose soil (see 1) with extra humus is fine, but fertilize about every three weeks. Grow in a south window at normal house temperatures.

921. *Why is my shrimp plant so leggy?*

This is a natural tendency. Promote bushiness in a young plant by pinching out the tips of the shoots. Once a plant becomes leggy, you may as well give up on it. Take 4-inch tip cuttings, preferably about May, and raise new plants (see 130-133).

SIDERASIS FUSCATA

Small, tropical rosette plant with broad green leaves with soft red hairs and a silvery band down the center and lavender-blue flowers in spring

922. *Is siderasis recommended for growing indoors?*

Yes. Plant in general-purpose soil (see 1) with extra humus and grow at an east or west window at 60° to 70°F. Water when the soil surface is almost dry. Fertilize about once a month.

SINNINGIA

Tuberous-rooted gesneriads from Brazil. The best known species is S. *speciosa* (gloxinia), but several others with attractive foliage and delightful flowers are grown for winter, spring, or summer bloom. Two of the best are S. *regina,* with purple flowers and silver-veined leaves reddish underneath, and S. *pusilla,* only 2 inches tall with profuse lavender flowers

923. *Are the species sinningias grown like gloxinias?*

In exactly the same way (see 618-647). Normally they bloom in spring and summer, but like gloxinias they can be brought into flower much earlier in the year. Allow about four months from planting to bloom. After flowering, let the tubers rest several months before starting into growth again.

SMITHIANTHA (temple bells)

Formerly called *Naegelia,* a rhizomatous gesneriad from Mexico with beautiful bell-shaped, winter flowers ranging from cream to red and large heart-shaped leaves covered with red or purple hairs or marked with red or purple veins.

924. *Can I grow smithiantha successfully in the house?*

Yes, grow like achimenes (see 166-172) in an east window with warmth, humidity, a good supply of moisture and fertilizer every two weeks.

925. *How are smithiantha rhizomes started?*

Use sterilized soil of equal parts loam, humus, and sand. Plant individual rhizomes in 2¼-inch pots or about three rhizomes to a 4-inch pot, with the rhizomes set on their sides about ½ inch below the surface. Water sparingly until plants are about 2 inches high. Keep pots in a warm, light (but not sunny) place to hasten growth.

926. *What do I do with my smithianthas when they stop blooming toward the end of February?*

Gradually withhold water until the foliage dies down. Then store the rhizomes in dry soil in their pots in a cool, dark place. Allow them to rest until summer before starting into growth again.

927. *A friend watered my smithiantha too much while I was away for several weeks and the plant now looks bad. Can it be pulled through to bloom?*

Perhaps not, but try cutting the tops back hard and repotting with careful arrangements for drainage. Keep somewhat on the dry side while new growth develops. This has worked for others.

928. *Can smithiantha be grown from seeds?*

From seeds, stem cuttings, leaf cuttings, the divided rhizomes, and even from the scales on the rhizomes. Sow the seeds or take cuttings in early spring and keep in a warm place.

SNAKE PLANT (*Sansevieria*)

Also called bowstring-hemp, African plant with thick, upright leaves striped or banded with yellow or light green and sometimes with spikes of yellow or white flowers in August

929. *What soil should I use for a snake plant?*

General-purpose mixture (see 1), with fertilizer only about every three months. This is a tough plant and easy to grow so long as you do not overwater it at the roots but do sponge off the leaves frequently.

930. *Will snake plant grow in dark rooms?*

It gets along in a dim light but does better in a fully light north window. If you put it outdoors in summer, keep on a covered porch or terrace.

931. *Can overwatering kill a snake plant? I can't figure what else I did to kill mine.*

It is definitely injured by too much water or by poor drainage, which may cause root rot. Watering once a week is usually enough, but when you do it, soak the soil thoroughly. It is advisable to water from below so that the deep roots will be well moistened. Never let the pot stand in a saucer full of water.

932. *How do I propagate the snake plant?*

Cut the leaves in 4-inch lengths and insert them, right side up as they grow, half their length in damp sand. Cover with polyethylene film to maintain humidity (see 133).

933. *I made leaf cuttings of a striped snake plant, but the new plants are solid green. Is this normal?*

Yes. To perpetuate variegated snake plants, propagate them by division of the fleshy roots.

SNOWDROP (*Galanthus*)

Spring bulb from Eurasia with nodding, bell-like, white flowers

934. *Can I force snowdrops for indoor bloom?*

Yes (see 148-152). Plant in general-purpose soil with the tops just below the surface, water, and store in a cold, dark place. Allow about eight weeks for roots to develop before bringing into a warm place.

935. *I tried to force snowdrops last year but although I followed the rules, I got poor results. Why might this have been?*

Possibly bulbs were out of the ground too long before you planted them. Snowdrops should be planted just as soon as they are available.

SPANISH SHAWL (*Schizocentron elegans*)

Creeping Mexican perennial with small leaves and reddish-purple, 1-inch flowers in spring

936. *Why doesn't my Spanish shawl bloom well?*

This is ordinarily not a difficult plant, since it requires only general-purpose soil (see 1), warmth, plenty of water, and bright light without much sun. If you are satisfying these needs and still not getting good bloom, then check the humidity of the room. For some reason, many people have no trouble with Spanish shawl in a dry atmosphere, but others do. So try increasing the humidity by spraying the foliage frequently with water and keeping the pots in pebble-filled saucers (see 92).

937. *When should I prune a Spanish shawl plant?*

After it is through blooming in the summer, cut it back about a half. You can propagate some of the cuttings in moist sand.

SPATHIPHYLLUM

Perennial from tropical America with long, lance-shaped leaves and long-lasting white spathes forming a flower like a calla lily from about Easter well into autumn

938. *Will I have difficulty growing spathiphyllum in the house?*

Not if you follow the simple rules: Plant in general-purpose soil (see 1) with a double quantity of humus. Maintain 65° to 75°F temperature and a high humidity. Keep soil evenly moist except from November through January when water should be reduced. Grow in an east window.

SPIDER PLANT (*Chlorophytum elatum*)

Incorrectly called *Anthericum,* a South African plant with narrow, sometimes white- or yellow-marked leaves and long trailing stems with clusters of plantlets at the tips

939. *Is spider plant an easy one to grow indoors?*

Very easy. It needs a moist general-purpose soil (see 1) and average indoor temperatures. It will grow in sun but does equally well in a north window. Nice for a high plant shelf with the little new plants dripping over the edge.

940. *How should I propagate spider plant?*

You can divide the roots or layer the stems. Just pin a stem down in a nearby pot of soil and keep moist. When roots develop, cut off the stem (see 142).

STAPELIA (carrion flower)

South African succulents with thick, short, four-sided, erect stems that grow rather haphazardly and with no true leaves, but with spectacular, variously colored summer flowers that are sometimes evil smelling

941. *Can stapelias be grown the same way as other succulents?*

Yes (see 957-965). Give warmth, sun (except in summer, when light shading is needed), fresh air, and a moderate amount of moisture.

942. *Some of the branches of my stapelia grew a lot and then developed rot. What would cause this?*

Probably too much water and perhaps too much fertilizer. In winter, water just enough to prevent shriveling. In summer, water only when the soil becomes dry on the surface, and then thoroughly. Use a porous soil and plenty of drainage material to prevent waterlogging.

943. *I am told that the different varieties of stapelia require different types of soil. Is this true?*

Yes. Those with a smooth skin do well in standard succulent soil (see 957); those with a velvety skin need a much richer mixture: 2 parts humus (mixed with manure if available), 1 part loam, and 1 part sand.

STAR JASMINE (*Trachelospermum jasminoides*)

Also called Confederate jasmine, tall, woody Chinese vine with leathery foliage and clusters of small, fragrant, star-shaped, white blooms from spring through fall

944. *How is the star jasmine grown?*

Provide a general-purpose soil (see 1) and water when the soil feels dry. Grow at a south window in normal house temperatures, but note that plants under two years of age need somewhat more warmth than old specimens. Train up cords or trellises.

945. *Should star jasmine be put outdoors in summer?*

Yes, plunge the pot in partial shade near a fence or trellis to which the stems can be trained. Don't be tempted to plant directly in the garden, because tops and roots will quickly get away from you. This is a fast grower.

STAR OF BETHLEHEM (*Ornithogalum*)

One species also called chincherinchee, a widely distributed, tall, bulbous plant with winter and spring clusters of white flowers, the shape of which varies with the species

946. *How do I handle star of Bethlehem bulbs?*

Plant 1 inch deep, three to a 5-inch pot, in autumn. Use general-purpose soil (see 1). Water regularly and keep in a light, cool place for about 6 weeks. Then when growth is well started, bring to a sunny window.

STRAWBERRY GERANIUM (*Saxifraga sarmentosa*)

Also called strawberry begonia, Aaron's beard, beefsteak saxifrage, or mother of thousands. Trailing Chinese and Japanese plant that puts out runners like the strawberry with tiny plants at the tip, and has interesting foliage and panicles of white summer flowers

947. *Is strawberry geranium easy to grow?*

Yes. Use general-purpose soil (see 1). Grow in a bright but not too sunny window (north and east exposures are fine). Keep soil moist and temperature low (see 948).

948. *Why do I have so much trouble with red spiders on my strawberry geranium?*

You are probably growing the plant in too hot and dry a room. This plant prefers cool temperatures—down as low as 50°F—and fair humidity.

949. *Are strawberry geraniums propagated from runners?*

Yes, in spring just pin a runner down on the moist soil of a nearby pot and cut it off after roots develop (see 142). If a runner already has a plantlet at the tip, you can also nip off the little fellow and pot it directly in general-purpose soil.

STREPTOCARPUS (cape primrose)

South African gesneriad with tubular flowers in a wide range of colors mostly in autumn and winter

950. *Why is the bloom so poor on my streptocarpus?*

Something is wrong with the culture. This plant requires a loose, humusy soil (equal parts loam, humus, and sand) kept evenly moist and fertilized once a month. Grow at a warm east or west window and keep the atmosphere fairly humid.

951. *Could streptocarpus be grown on a cool sun porch?*

Unlike other gesneriads, streptocarpus does not require more or less constant warmth. It will grow on your sun porch if the temperature does not drop below 50°F at night. During the day, the temperature should be from the high 60's up to 75°F.

952. *My streptocarpus was growing well and then suddenly seemed to come to a standstill. Why?*

It probably outgrew its pot. The fibrous roots of this plant are lusty, and repotting is therefore required about once a year.

953. *How is streptocarpus propagated?*

Sow seeds in spring or summer. Or take leaf cuttings (see 140) from actively growing plants and insert in moist sand. Some plants also form offsets which can be separated and planted directly in potting soil. Upright species can also be propagated by stem cuttings.

954. *Is it possible to get continuous bloom from a streptocarpus?*

Some species bloom for months at a stretch; S. *saxorum*, for instance, goes on for more than six months. But for continuous bloom, make successive sowings of seed through the year. It takes six to nine months from sowing to flowering.

STROBILANTHES DYERIANUS

Burmese shrub to 3 feet with leaves that are iridescent purple and small violet flower spikes in winter

955. *Isn't strobilanthes difficult to raise indoors?*

Not if it has warmth (65° to 75°F), an abundance of humidity (spray foliage frequently with water), constant moisture at the roots, and diffused sun. Pot in general-purpose soil (see 1) with an extra quantity of humus.

956. *My year-old strobilanthes is getting weedy. How can I restore its shape?*

Don't try; this happens to all strobilanthes. Better start some young plants in spring or summer from stem cuttings.

SUCCULENTS

Plants from arid areas that either store water or can get along with very little. These questions deal with succulents (but not cacti) in general. Specific succulents included in this book are *Agave, Aloe, Bryophyllum, Crassula*, crown of thorns, *Echeveria, Haworthia*, houseleek, ice plant, *Kalanchoe*, little pickles, living stones, rosary vine, *Sedum*, and *Stapelia*

957. *I brought home sandy soil from the desert and planted succulents in it, but they are doing badly. Why?*

Indoors, succulents need somewhat better soil, and they must also have excellent drainage. Mix loam, leaf mold, and sand in equal parts. Add a little gravel or finely broken flower pot. For drainage, fill the container one-quarter full of shards.

958. *Should succulents be in a south window?*

Yes. They need all the sun they can get indoors. These

plants, for the most part, come from deserts where they are exposed to searing sun.

959. *How much heat will succulents stand?*

When in a period of active growth they can stand higher temperatures than those in the normal home. While resting, they can stand temperatures down to 50°F, or even lower, and they should be watered very little.

960. *How often should succulents be watered?*

In spring and summer, when most succulents make growth, water whenever soil feels dry, and soak it all the way through. In fall, gradually reduce watering, and in winter, give just enough to keep plants from shriveling (but don't worry if the lowest leaves dry up). If you buy a budded plant from a florist in winter, however, consider it in a state of active growth and water regularly.

961. *With succulents is there a relationship between heat and watering?*

The lower the temperature, the less water required by succulents. The higher the temperature, the more water required. This applies not only to succulents, but to most plants.

962. *Do succulents need to be fertilized?*

Very little—no more than small amounts of dilute solutions once a month when the plants are growing actively (usually from early spring through fall). The best fertilizers for succulents are low in nitrogen, higher in phosphorus and potassium.

963. *Can succulents be put outside in summer?*

Yes, plunge the pots in the garden and be sure to put

a thick layer of gravel or hard cinders under the pots to provide drainage. Most should be placed in full sun (but see 82); but some, such as stapelia, require light shading. If you do not know how much sun a particular plant can take, keep a close watch over it and if you see the least sign of burning, give it some shading immediately.

964. *How are succulents propagated?*

Most of them from stem cuttings in spring or summer. Put these in a dry, shaded, airy place for several days or even several weeks until the cuts dry over and form calluses. Then plant very shallowly in barely damp sand. Keep in filtered shade at 75°F and water very little until the cuttings begin to plump up and show fresh color.

965. *Can succulents be propagated from seeds?*

Yes. Sow seeds in spring or early summer in a flat or pot of finely shredded sphagnum moss or in sifted, sterilized general-purpose soil (see 1) with a double quantity of sand. Press in firmly and sprinkle shredded sphagnum on top. Water from below, cover with glass, and keep in a warm, light (but not sunny) place until seeds germinate. To avoid damping-off—a common problem with succulent seedlings—spray soil and seedlings lightly with a solution of Semesan.

SWEDISH IVY (*Plectranthus*)

Creeping and trailing plants from Natal with scalloped, round leaves, often variegated, and inconspicuous lavender flowers in spring

966. *Would Swedish ivy be a good fast-growing plant for a hanging basket?*

Yes, it trails prettily and is also a good creeper. It requires average attention: general-purpose soil (see 1) which is watered thoroughly when it feels dry, normal house temperatures, humidity, sun, or shade.

967. *What is the easiest way to propagate Swedish ivy?*

All ways are easy. Stems touching the soil will root naturally. Or start stem cuttings in water or moist sand. Or divide the roots.

SWEET OLIVE (*Osmanthus fragrans*)

Slow-growing shrub from southeast Asia up to 4 feet with glossy leaves and tiny, very fragrant white flowers in winter

968. *What is the right temperature for the sweet olive?*

In the 50's; it does not do well in warmer rooms. Otherwise it is undemanding, requiring only a general-purpose soil (see 1), which should be kept evenly moist, and good light—as in an east or west window. In the summer, move outside into filtered sun. In late summer, make cuttings of half-ripe wood.

SWEET POTATO (*Ipomoea batatas*)

Tropical garden vegetable grown indoors for its excellent trailing foliage

969. *How can I grow a sweet potato in the window garden?*

Set the tuber in the neck of a narrow jar of water so that about half of the fat end sticks out. Let about 1 inch of the lower end reach into the water. Add a lump of charcoal to keep water sweet. Growth should start quickly and continue for a long time in an east or west window.

970. *Why didn't the sweet potato I planted in a jar of water ever grow?*

If you bought the potato at a grocery, it probably had been cured. Such tubers often do not develop roots. Select an uncured tuber or, if you can't find one, pick out one that has started to sprout.

SYNGONIUM

Tropical American climber or trailer with beautifully shaped, sometimes variegated leaves resembling the philodendron's but identifiable by a milky stem juice

971. *How much light, moisture, and humidity does syngonium demand?*

Grow in an east or west window or a fully light north window at normal house temperatures but with above-average humidity. Provide a general-purpose soil (see 1) and keep it evenly moist.

TILLANDSIA

Tropical American bromeliads, all air plants of various shapes, many with basal rosettes and small, cuplike flowers in many colors in winter

972. *Should I use the bromeliad potting soil for tillandsia?*

Since this is an air plant, it will grow only in osmunda fiber. You can even grow it by enclosing the roots in a bit of osmunda and wiring them to a board. But you can pot the plant like other bromeliads if you prefer.

973. *When should I water tillandsia?*

In spring and summer give plenty of water (see 344); but in winter, when it is partially dormant, reduce the supply. For full details about the culture of this plant see 342-353.

TULIP (*Tulipa*)

Gorgeous spring-blooming old world bulbs in white, pink, red, yellow, orange, and purple—excellent for forcing

974. *Which tulip varieties are recommended for forcing?*

Of the many that can be forced, the best are usually indicated in catalogs by a special symbol. In general, the single and double earlies and the Mendels do very well.

975. *How are tulips forced for indoor winter bloom?*

See 148-152. Plant top-size bulbs about ½ inch apart in 6- to 8-inch pots or bulb pans in October or November. For a succession of indoor bloom, bring in from cold storage at two-week intervals after roots fill containers.

UMBRELLA PLANT (*Cyperus alternifolius*)

African plant up to 4 feet with slender stems bearing umbrella-shaped clusters of glossy leaves at the ends

976. *How much water does an umbrella plant need?*

A great deal because this is a bog plant. You can keep the soil almost soaking wet or let the pot stand in a saucer of water. Given enough moisture, this plant does well in sun or very light shade. Propagate stem cuttings in water and when they root, pot in general-purpose soil (see 1).

UMBRELLA TREE (*Schefflera actinophylla*)

Fast-growing tree up to 10 feet from the South Pacific with umbrella-shaped leaf clusters variegated creamy white

977. *What is the proper treatment for the umbrella tree?*

Use general-purpose soil (see 1) and water thoroughly

when surface feels dry. Grow at an east or west window in normal house temperatures. Move outdoors into partial shade in summer. When the plant becomes too large, air-layer the stem (see 141) and throw the old tree out.

VELTHEIMIA

Tall, bulbous plant from South Africa with handsome, long leaves and a tight, pointed cluster of tubular, rosy-pink flowers in December through April

978. *How is a veltheimia bulb planted?*

Plant half in and half out of general-purpose soil (see 1) in a 6-inch pot in September through December. Water sparingly and keep in a good light until growth starts, then increase supply and move to a sunny window. Flowers appear in about three months.

979. *Can veltheimia flowers be made to last longer?*

When buds are ready to open, move the plant out of direct sun but keep in fully open light. The flowers will open and last about six weeks.

980. *How do I carry over a veltheimia bulb?*

When flowering is over, cut off the flower stalk and gradually withhold water until the foliage dies down. Then store the bulb, in its pot, in a cool, dark place. Start into growth again in the fall.

VELVET PLANT (*Gynura aurantiaca*)

Handsome Javanese plant up to 30 inches with large, oval leaves covered with hairs that make the foliage look like purple velvet

981. *What soil and watering does the velvet plant require?*

Plant in general-purpose soil (see 1) with some dried manure for enrichment if it is available. Keep soil evenly moist and spray foliage frequently to provide humidity.

982. *Why aren't the leaves of my velvet plant more colorful? The plant looks healthy.*

Perhaps you have not given it the sun or warmth needed to bring out best color. Grow in a south window at 70°F.

983. *Why doesn't my velvet plant bloom?*

The velvet plant's yellow or orange flowers usually appear only on plants that are a couple of years old. Unfortunately, such plants are pretty leggy. Many people therefore grow velvet plants only for their handsome foliage and start new plants from cuttings every summer.

VENUS FLY TRAP (*Dionaea muscipula*)

Low-growing insectivorous plant with folding leaves from the Carolinas

984. *How does the Venus fly trap catch flies?*

The folding, shell-like leaves with long marginal "teeth" lie open until a fly lands within them. Then the trap springs shut and remains so for about ten days until the fly is digested.

985. *How can I grow the Venus fly trap?*

Plant in sphagnum moss or a mixture of peat moss and sand in a 3- to 5-inch pot. Keep well watered—this plant can stand in a saucer of water—and grow at about 60°F. The plant does exceptionally well in a terrarium.

986. *Is a north window the right exposure for Venus fly trap?*

No. The plant requires a fair amount of sun, as in an east or southeast window, and also a humid atmosphere.

987. *My Venus fly trap seemed to weaken after it flowered. Was it wrong to let it bloom?*

This plant is not too easy to grow, and flowering does weaken it. Next time, cut off the flower stalks as they develop.

WANDERING JEW

Common name for two similar trailing plants from Central America grown for their foliage. *Tradescantia fluminensis* has pale green or striped leaves and white flowers in spring and summer. *Zebrina pendula* has foliage that is reddish-purple underneath and purple flowers in spring and summer

988. *Is the wandering Jew plant easy to grow in the house?*

Very easy. It needs no more light than that of a north window and is not particular about temperature. The only demand is a fair amount of moisture at the roots. Plant in general-purpose soil (see 1) and fertilize occasionally.

989. *Can I grow wandering Jew in water only?*

Yes, and you can also root cuttings easily in a jar of water.

WAX PLANT (*Hoya carnosa*)

Climbing tropical vine with fleshy leaves sometimes variegated pink or white and small, fragrant, waxy white flowers from June through September

990. *What soil does the wax plant need?*

Equal parts loam, humus, and sand make a good mixture,

but actually it doesn't seem to make much difference what you use. People have even grown this plant successfully in pure sphagnum moss.

991. *How should a wax plant be handled to produce maximum bloom?*

In fall and early winter, grow the plant in a cool (50° to 60°F), light place and water just enough to keep leaves from shriveling. In February, move to a 70°F, sunny place; water freely; fertilize about every three weeks, and spray the foliage with water every week.

992. *Why doesn't my wax plant bloom well?*

Assuming that you have given it good growing conditions (see 991), your problem may be that the plant is not old enough—it may take two years for one to flower—or the pot is too big. The wax plant blooms well only when it is pot-bound.

993. *Is it correct not to remove the little stems that bear flowers on wax plants?*

Quite correct; these spurs will produce flowers again.

994. *How are wax plants trained?*

They climb by means of aerial rootlets, so give them something rough to hold on to. A piece of wood covered with bark is excellent. Or you can also let them clamber up a lattice or strings.

995. *In the summer can I put my wax plant outdoors?*

This is ideal treatment. Plunge the pot in partial sun and keep it well watered. Fertilize every three weeks.

996. *I tried propagating wax plants from leaf cuttings, as I was told, but it was a slow process. Aren't there better ways?*

Yes. Layer the stems (see 141) or take tip cuttings in spring.

XANTHOSOMA

Tropical American foliage plant with large leaves veined in different colors

997. *How is xanthosoma potted?*

Use a general-purpose soil (see 1) with extra humus, and keep it moist. Provide very good drainage and a pot not much larger than the fleshy roots.

998. *Does xanthosoma require high humidity and sun?*

High humidity is essential to good growth (this is primarily a greenhouse plant) but a great deal of sun is not. Grow in an east window or a fully bright north one.

999. *Why did my xanthosoma drop its leaves?*

Probably because the room was cold. Generally speaking, this plant requires 65°F minimum, although one species, *X. violaceum,* tolerates several degrees less.

1000. *How can I reproduce xanthosoma?*

Divide the roots in summer and be sure that each piece has a growing eye or sprout.

ZEPHYR LILY (*Zephyranthes grandiflora*)

Also called fairy lily, a small tropical American bulbous

plant with graceful red or pink, lilylike flowers in winter, spring, or summer, depending on when they are planted

1001. How do I plant zephyr lilies?

In general-purpose soil (see 1) with a double quantity of sand. Plant the bulbs, eight in a 10-inch pot, just below the soil surface. Put the pot in a sunny window and keep soil moist. Flowering starts in about five weeks.

SECTION **3**

Useful Lists

WHERE TO GROW . . . WHAT TO GROW . . . WHERE TO BUY

Plants for North Windows

Mainly foliage plants, these will do well if grown in a fully light north window.

Amonum cardamon
Aralia
Ardisia crispa
Aspidistra
Babys-tears
Chinese evergreen
Ctenanthe
Dichorisandra
English ivy
Fatshedera
Fatsia japonica
Fiddle-leaf fig
Hoffmannia
Holly fern
Kangaroo vine
Kentia
Maidenhair fern
Monstera
Nephthytis afzeli
Norfolk Island pine
Peperomia
Philodendron
Pick-a-back plant
Rabbits-foot fern
Redwood burl
Rubber plant
Snake plant
Spider plant
Staghorn fern
Strawberry geranium
Table fern
Wandering Jew

Plants for South Windows

If you have an unobstructed south window that gets more than 5 hours of sun a day, these plants—almost entirely flowering types—will thrive, and should bloom their heads off.

Abelia grandiflora Edward Goucher
Acacia
Acalypha
Agave
Allamanda cathartica Hendersoni
Aloe
Amaryllis
Anemone coronaria
Apostle plant
Astrophytum
Azalea
Bird of paradise
Blood leaf
Bougainvillea glabra
Bouvardia
Bowiea
Browallia speciosa major
Bryophyllum
Calla lily
Callistemon lanceolatus
Camellia japonica
Cattleya
Chrysanthemum
Cigar flower
Clerodendron Thomsonae
Clivia
Coleus
Crassula
Crocus
Croton
Crown of thorns
Chionodoxa
Daffodil
Dendrobium
Diosma ericoides
Dumpling cactus
Dwarf banana
Easter lily cactus
Echeveria
Epidendrum
Eranthemum nervosum
Fame flower
Firecracker vine
Flowering maple
Freesia
Gardenia
Geranium
Gloriosa
Golden barrel cactus
Grapefruit
Grape hyacinth
Haemanthus
Haworthia
Heliotrope

Houseleek
Hyacinth
Hydrangea
Ice plant
Indoor oak
Iris
Ixia
Jacobean lily
Jasmine
Jerusalem cherry
Josephs-coat
Kalanchoe
Kenilworth ivy
Lachenalia
Lantana
Lemon
Lily
Lily-of-the-valley
Little pickles
Living stones
Madagascar jasmine
Marguerite
Mexican foxglove
Morning glory
Myrtle
Narcissus
Natal plum
Necklace vine
Notocactus
Oleander
Orange
Orange browallia
Oxalis
Passion flower
Patience
Peanut cactus
Pentas lanceolata
Pepper
Peristrophe angustifolia aureo-variegata
Phaius
Pincushion cactus
Pineapple
Pittosporum tobira
Poinsettia
Pomegranate
Ranunculus
Rebutia
Rose
Rosemary
Scilla
Sedum
Shrimp plant
Sensitive plant
Snowdrop
Stapelia
Star jasmine
Star of Bethlehem
Tulip
Umbrella plant
Vanda
Veltheimia
Velvet plant
Wax plant
Zephyr lily

Plants for East or West Windows

Plants to grow in east or west windows—both flowering and foliage types—are those that need no more than four hours of sun a day to do well. Generally east windows are preferable to west because they are cooler.

Acanthostachys strobilacea
Achimenes
Acorus gramineus variegatus
Aechmea
Aeschynanthus
African violet
Alocasia
Alpinia
Amazon lily
Aphelandra squarrosa Louisae
Ardisia crispa
Asparagus
Australian silk oak
Avocado
Babys-tears
Basket grass
Begonia
Bertolonia
Billbergia nutans
Birds-nest fern
Bletilla
Boston fern
Brunfelsia calycina floribunda
California pitcher plant
Caladium
Calathea
Callisia
Christmas cactus
Columnea
Costus
Creeping fig
Cryptanthus
Cyanotis
Cyclamen
Dumb cane
Easter cactus
Episcia
Euonymus japonicus
Flame-of-the-woods
Flaming sword
Flamingo flower
Fuchsia
Genista
German ivy
Gloxinera
Gloxinia
Gold dust plant
Grape ivy
Ground ivy
Guzmania
Justicia extensa
Kampfaeria roscoeana

Kings-crown
Kohleria
Leopard plant
Maranta
Miniature holly
Moses-in-the-cradle
Moss
Nautilocalyx
Neoregelia
Night-blooming cereus
Orchid cactus
Pandanus
Pellionia
Phalaenopsis
Pilea
Pitcher plant
Pothos
Primrose
Pseuderanthemum
Pygmy date palm
Rechsteineria
Red ivy
Rhektophyllum mirabile
Rhipsalis
Rosary vine
Ruellia makoyana
Swedish ivy
Sanchezia nobilis glaucophylla
Serissa foetida variegata
Siderasis fuscata
Sinningia
Smithiantha
Spanish shawl
Spathiphyllum
Streptocarpus
Striped chin cactus
Strobilanthes dyerianus
Sweet olive
Sweet potato
Syngonium
Tillandsia
Umbrella tree
Venus fly trap
Xanthosoma

Plants Requiring Temperatures Below 60°F

Abelia grandiflora Edward Goucher
Acacia
Acorus gramineus variegatus
Anemone coronaria
Asparagus
Australian silk oak
Azalea
Bouvardia
California pitcher plant
Camellia
Cineraria
Cyclamen
English ivy

Euonymus japonicus
Flowering maple
Freesia
Gold dust plant
Hydrangea
Ixia
Jerusalem cherry
Lily
Marguerite
Myrtle
Norfolk Island pine
Oleander
Pepper
Pittosporum tobira
Primrose
Ranunculus
Strawberry geranium
Sweet olive

Flowers for Every Month

You can have fresh, gay color in your home every month of the year if you pick the right plants and start them at the right time. Here are just a few possibilities for each month.

October-November

African violet
Anemone
Begonia, wax
Bouvardia
Campanula isophylla
Chrysanthemum
Geranium
Lachenalia
Morning glory
Narcissus
Ranunculus
Shrimp plant
Sweet olive

December

African violet
Begonia, wax and Christmas
Bouvardia
Christmas cactus
Crown of thorns
Cyclamen
Geranium
Hyacinth, French Roman
Kalanchoe
Lily-of-the-valley
Narcissus
Poinsettia
Sweet olive

January

African violet
Begonia, wax and Christmas
Christmas cactus
Crown of thorns
Cyclamen
Geranium
Freesia
Hyacinth
Kalanchoe
Lily-of-the-valley
Narcissus
Oxalis
Patience
Poinsettia
Primrose
Shrimp plant
Star of Bethlehem
Sweet olive
Veltheimia

February-March

African violet
Amaryllis
Apostle plant
Azalea
Begonia, wax and others
Calla lily
Camellia
Christmas cactus
Clivia
Cyclamen
Daffodil
Easter cactus
Firecracker vine
Flaming sword
Flamingo flower
Freesia
Gardenia
Geranium
Gloxinia
Hyacinth
Jacobean lily
Lemon
Marguerite
Orange
Orchids
Patience
Rose
Spathiphyllum
Star of Bethlehem
Tulip
Veltheimia

April

African violet
Amaryllis
Begonia, wax
Calla lily

Crown of thorns
Easter cactus
Easter lily
Flaming sword
Flamingo flower
Gardenia
Geranium
Gloxinia
Hydrangea
Ixia
Jacobean lily
Patience
Primrose
Spathiphyllum
Star jasmine

May-Summer (the sky is the limit)

Abelia
Achimenes
African violet
Begonia
Bird of paradise
Cacti
Chinese hibiscus
Fuchsia
Geranium
Gloriosa
Jasmine
Kaempferia roscoeana
Strawberry geranium
Succulents
Wax plant

Fine Foliage Plants

These have much to offer with their interesting, attractively shaped and arranged foliage that is sometimes very colorful. How could we get along without them? Most need only good light, but some require considerable sun to bring out their colors.

Acorus gramineus variegatus
Agave
Alocasia
Amonum cardamon
Aralia sieboldi
Asparagus
Aspidistra
Australian silk oak
Avocado
Babys-tears
Basket grass
Begonia, rex
Bertolonia
Blood leaf

Bowiea
Bryophyllum
Caladium
Calathea
California pitcher plant
Callisia
Coleus
Creeping fig
Croton
Ctenanthe
Cyanotis
Dracaena
Dumb cane
English ivy
Euonymus japonicus
Fatshedera
Ferns
Fiddle-leaf fig
German ivy
Grapefruit
Grape ivy
Ground ivy
Hoffmannia
Indoor oak
Josephs-coat
Justicia extensa
Maranta
Monstera deliciosa
Necklace vine
Neoregelia (some)
Nephthytis afzeli
Norfolk Island pine
Palms
Pandanus
Pellionia
Peperomia
Philodendron
Pick-a-back plant
Pilea
Pineapple
Pothos
Redwood burl
Rhektophyllum mirabile
Rubber plant
Sensitive plant
Snake plant
Spider plant
Sweet potato
Syngonium
Tillandsia
Umbrella plant
Umbrella tree
Velvet plant

Fragrant Plants for Indoors

These look pretty, grow well, and give off a delicious fragrance.

Amonum cardamon
Bouvardia
Diosma ericoides
Eucharis grandiflora

Freesia
Gardenia
Genista
Geranium, scented-leaved
Heliotrope
Hyacinth
Jasmine officinala grandiflorum
Kaempferia roscoeana
Lemon
Lily-of-the-valley
Madagascar jasmine
Narcissus
Natal plum
Night-blooming cereus
Orange
Pittosporum tobira
Rosemary
Star jasmine
Stephanotis
Sweet olive
Wax plant

Fruiting Plants for the Home

Always a delight, these plants will hold their fruit for a long time if you keep them cool (about 60°F as a general rule), water regularly and deeply, and mist the tops frequently.

Ardisia crispa
Dwarf banana (rare)
Gold dust plant
Jerusalem cherry
Lemon
Natal plum
Orange
Pepper
Pomegranate

Climbing Vines

Lovely plants to train up walls or around windows to give a big show of fresh greenery and, in many cases, color as well.

Allamanda cathartica hendersoni
Asparagus
Bougainvillea glabra
Bowiea
Clerodendron thomsonae
Creeping fig
English ivy
Firecracker vine
German ivy
Gloriosa
Grape ivy

Kangaroo vine
Madagascar jasmine
Monstera deliciosa
Morning glory
Necklace vine
Nephthytis afzeli
Night-blooming cereus
Orange browallia
Passion flower
Philodendron
Rhektophyllum mirabile
Star jasmine
Syngonium
Wax plant

Hanging Plants

Plant them in a hanging container or a wall bracket and they will droop prettily and give an airy grace to any room.

Acanthostachys strobilacea
Achimenes
Aeschynanthus
African violets (some)
Begonias, basket
Browallia speciosa major
Campanula isophylla
Columnea
Cyanotis
Episcia
Geranium, ivy
Kenilworth ivy
Kohleria
Orchid cactus
Oxalis
Pellionia
Peristrophe angustifolia aureo-variegata
Philodendron
Red ivy
Rhipsalis
Rosary vine
Ruellia makoyana
Sedum (donkey's tail)
Spanish shawl
Strawberry geranium
Swedish ivy
Sweet potato
Syngonium
Wandering Jew

Plants That Take Care of Themselves

These demand relatively little attention—you can take a vacation for three or four days or even a little longer, and when you come back they will be doing as well as ever. But don't stretch their possibilities too far.

Aspidistra
Australian silk oak
Avocado
Basket grass
Bromeliads
Cacti, desert
Chinese evergreen
Cigar flower
Creeping fig
Dracaena
Dumb cane
Euonymus japonicus
Fatshedera
Fiddle-leaf fig
German ivy
Grape ivy
Ground ivy
Hoffmannia
Kangaroo vine
Kenilworth ivy
Monstera deliciosa
Moses-in-the-cradle
Philodendron
Pick-a-back plant
Pothos
Redwood burl
Rubber plant
Snake plant
Spider plant
Succulents
Swedish ivy
Sweet potato
Umbrella plant
Umbrella tree

Some Sources of House Plants

Alberts & Merkle Bros., U.S. Highway 1, Boynton Beach, Fla.
Tropical foliage plants, bromeliads, orchids
Antonelli Bros., 2545 Capitola Rd., Santa Cruz, Calif.
Gesneriads, begonias
Barrington Greenhouses, 860 Clements Bridge Rd., Barrington, N.J. Wide selection
Beahm Gardens, 2686 E. Paloma St., Pasadena, Calif.
Cacti, succulents
Buell's, Eastford, Conn.
African violets, gloxinias, gesneriads

California Jungle Gardens, 11977 San Vicente Blvd., Los Angeles, Calif. Tropical plants, bromeliads

Castles of Florida, Orlando, Fla.
Tropical plants, bromeliads

Country Greenhouses, Cook Hill Rd., Danielson, Conn.
Begonias, geraniums, miscellaneous

P. deJager & Sons, 188 Asbury St., South Hamilton, Mass.
Spring bulbs, amaryllis

Fantastic Gardens, 9550 SW 67th Ave., South Miami, Fla.
Bromeliads

Fischer Greenhouses, Linwood, N.J.
African violets

House of Plants, 26 Hotchkiss St. S., Binghamton, N.Y.
Gesneriads

Johnson Cactus Gardens, P.O. Box 458, Paramount, Calif.
Cacti and succulents

Lager & Hurrell, 426 Morris Ave., Summit, N.J.
Orchids

Logee's Greenhouses, 55 North St., Danielson, Conn.
Wide selection

Merry Gardens, Camden, Me.
Wide selection

Holmes C. Miller, 280 W. Portola Ave., Los Altos, Calif.
Geraniums

Oakhurst Gardens, P.O. Box 444, Arcadia, Calif.
Wide selection

Pauer's Greenhouses, Rt. 1, Box 184, Waukesha, Wis.
Wide selection

Julius Roehrs Co., Rutherford, N.J.
Wide selection

Schmidt Nursery, 355 Lambert Ave., Palo Alto, Calif.
Fuchsias

Tinari Greenhouses, Bethayres, Pa.
African violets, episcias
Wilson Bros., Roachdale, Ind.
Geraniums
Yoars House Plant Nursery, Bunker Hill, Ind.
Begonias, miscellaneous

Index

Numbers refer to questions unless pages are indicated